An Introduction to Nigerian Upstream Oil and Gas Management

The Role in the Middle

Jide Akindele-Ojo

Copyright ©2018 **Jide Akindele-Ojo**

All rights reserved. No part of this publication may be reproduced or transmitted in any form or by any means, electronic, mechanical, photocopying, recording or otherwise, or stored in any retrieval system of any nature without the written permission of the copyright holder and the publisher.

Published in Nigeria by

Impart Oil and Gas Limited
1 Agbeke Rotinwa Close
Dolphin Extension, Ikoyi.
Email: info@impartoilandgas.com
Tel: +234 (0) 908 000 1123

ISBN: 978-978-968-569-1

Printed by
Detailz Graphix Limited
Ground Floor, Block C,
Adebowale House,
150, Ikorodu Road,
Onipanu, Lagos.
Tel: +234 803 322 5125

DEDICATION

This book is dedicated to the Divine Essence, to whom I owe my existence and abilities. This offering is to the self-existent Creator and all of creation which attests to His immutable existence.

To posterity and a legacy of excellence in an industry filled with a constellation of stellar performers.

To all who have gone before and blazed the trail, and to those coming after.

ACKNOWLEDGEMENTS

Every created being must endeavour to leave a good legacy. I am, therefore, intentional in writing this book. Adding value was intentional and the ultimate goal became clearer with time.

I acknowledge that this work is made possible because of the numerous seconds, minutes, hours, days, months, years, and decades that God has kept me safe and blessed.

I have received immeasurable support from Debbie: my friend, companion, and wife. Thank you for insisting that I write both my first and this second book. I am now more certain than ever that you are an angelic helper in human form.

To industry leaders, mentors, colleagues and contributors mentioned in this book: I trust that the time and effort invested in me have produced good fruit. You have been my inspiration.

Succeeding generations demand of us a good legacy, and rightfully so. Together, we can make a difference.

FOREWORD

Over the past decade working as an independent consultant, I have navigated the Oil and Gas industry with nostalgia. Before my retirement in 2008, I had worked in the Oil and Gas industry for some 28 years in various capacities but mostly as a Geoscientist both in Nigeria and some other locations in the diaspora. It was usually left to the top echelon and part of the middle management teams to straddle the thin, and sometimes invisible line, to determine the technical and financial importance of projects in projects management and delivery.

The typical human mind takes decisions based on heuristics judgement. Thus, one would assume that a prospective field with robustness as shown in the dataset from proven fields, proximity and presence of anomalies indicates the presence of drillable economic minerals. While this may be correct most of the time, it is not always a fool-proof assumption.

As a result, this corporate mind set limits the effectiveness of the middle management cadre. Their in-depth knowledge on the specific subject matter is recognised at a particular phase in the decision-making process. However, limited knowledge in other relevant aspects pertinent to arriving at a robust solution means that they are not able to take effective and practical decisions.

This book, An Introduction to Nigerian Upstream Oil and Gas Management reveals the latent gaps that may be causing hindrances in decision making and achieving set goals in Oil and Gas Organisations in Nigeria. The importance of a corporate governance structure, which when applied will assist companies to have a well-coordinated performance monitoring system, improve project quality delivery and achieve their corporate objectives, is illustrated in this book. Worthy of note is the analysis of the two-way Management Information Flow network, which highlights the relationship between credibility and the attitude of Managers and the impact on subordinates. This book challenges Managers to "Walk the Talk".

For prospective trainees, this material identifies the current gaps in the investment decision tree in the Oil and Gas industry. To succeed as a manager, you need to understand the complete value chain and the impact of each individual's attitude in the achievement of corporate objectives. I encourage you to apply the model proposed in this book, including the "4 Ds" soft skills, continually develop yourself which will in turn translate to growth and development for your company.

Jide Akindele-Ojo must be commended for this succinctly written professional work which is a compendium of his 38+ years of experience in the industry.

'Kunle Adegboye ADESIDA (Ph.D)

November, 2018

PREFACE

Approximately eight (8) years into my career, I came to a critical decision point. I had to determine if I wanted to continue as a Petroleum Geologist or branch off and mount the administrative ladder as a rookie Manager. This, as classy as it sounds, was confusing to me for the simple reason that there was really nothing in my experience up until that time which I could rely on to help me succeed in a managerial role.

It should be noted that the decision to recommend my move to the management cadre was not punitive. On the contrary, I was part of a select few who were chosen based on exemplary performance. Corporate leadership was on a drive for selected individuals to take on bigger challenges. Unfortunately, I had no clear line of sight to the arrival point (ultimate career potential) and it was therefore difficult to see an alignment with my departure point (current role and status). This is one of the most important parameters to ensuring success with any transitory intentions.

Permit me to fast forward to the present. I am today a leading executive in the oil and gas space; but I did not get there soon enough. In fact, I likely did not even attain my ultimate potential before leaving paid employment. The primary reason was a lack of mentorship. It was not customary to train technical professionals as Managers in my days. As I look around the industry some 38 years later, not much has changed. There are still about 80% of professionals staying on a technical trajectory with no diversification. It is an aberration not to expose technical professionals to leadership early enough. This leads to intrinsic error and the consequences can be rather profound.

This book is a product of intentionality and a burning desire to grow tomorrow's managers from the technical workforce through knowledge transfer today. The intention is to leave a sound legacy.

Effective learning is a function of whom or what we choose to learn from. We are limited in scope if we choose to learn only from our own mistakes. For example, I made my first error of judgement in leadership in 1994. It was not until later in life that I realised the error. I had quit my job to go on to what seemed like greener pastures at the time. With the benefit of hindsight, I see now that the decision I made then was capable of stunting my career growth.

The toughest person to lead is oneself. A good leader must first learn to lead themselves. I know now that wise people learn from the mistakes of others; the wisest of all learn from the successes of others. I can say today that I would not have made that career move in 1994 if I had mentorship.

Everyone needs a mentor. I have thus taken the initiative to serve others by writing this book. What makes this book special is that it affords me the opportunity to deliver mentorship in your space. This is a subject that we at Impart Oil and Gas Limited are very passionate about and which can make a difference in the business life of an organisation. Though this is a vast arena, we have customized this book to introduce management cadets to the Nigerian Upstream Oil and Gas environment.

The stakes are really high in leading others. When I came face-to-face with the consequences of my first leadership blunder, I wished someone had warned me about it. The stakes are even higher today. Like never before, there is more competition in the face of slimmer margins and increasing pressure to perform in today's markets.

Come on this introductory tour and let's talk about upstream Oil and Gas management. The book is organised in two parts. In Part One, we shall introduce you to some key facts and figures, definitions, industry nomenclature, petroleum fiscal systems and the concept of value chains. Part Two will appeal to most management theory devotees as it introduces the concept of functional roles, competencies as well as network functions. The section closes with suggested soft skills to keep your team in the leading position.

Welcome to an Introduction to Nigerian Upstream Oil and Gas Management: The Role in the Middle.

Jide Akindele-Ojo
2018

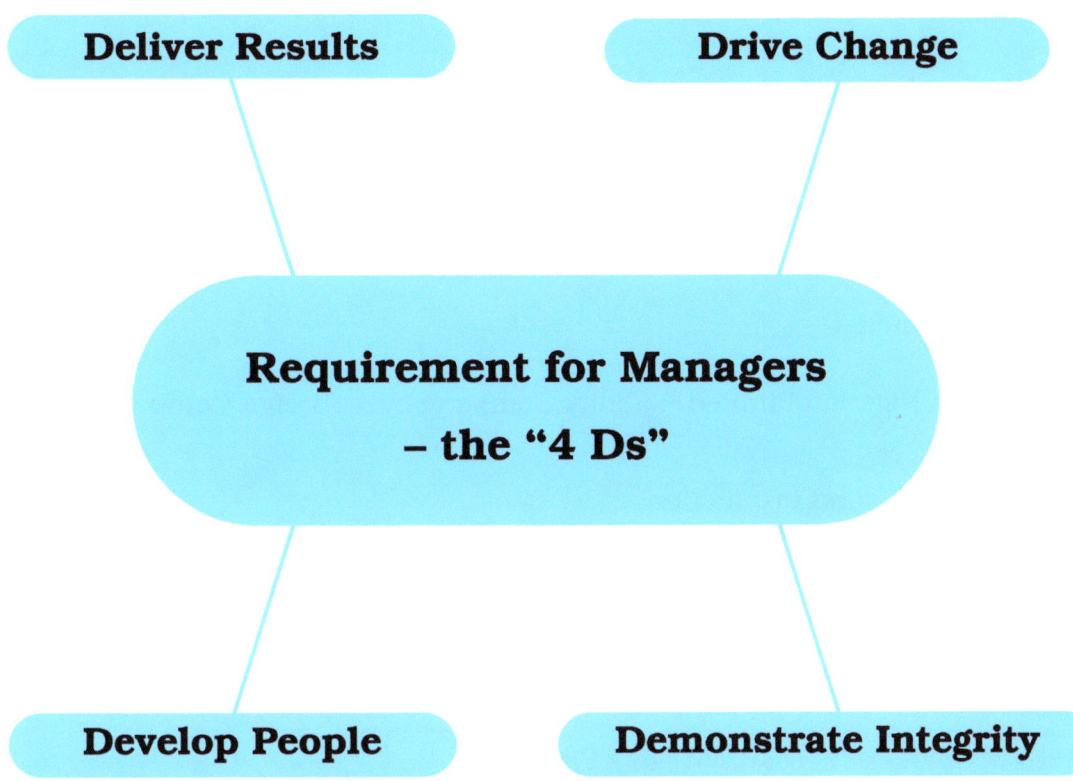

In this book, you will carry out some assignments in connection with your role as a manager. The intention is to help you increase the understanding of your role.

A good leader knows how to lead himself/herself.

A good leader will invest in evaluating and knowing themselves in order to lead himself/herself.

You will explore your roles in relation to normal and network environments. These analyses could form the basis for your Personal Development Plans.

The Leadership Development model referenced in this book has been compiled with theoretical input from Robert E. Quinn, Torod Strand, Yrjo Engelstroom and John C. Maxwell.

INTRODUCTION		5
1.1	Facts and Figures	6
NIGERIAN PETROLEUM LEGISLATION		9
2.1	The Department of Petroleum Resources (DPR)	9
2.2	The Petroleum Industry Bill	12
2.3	Licenses and Leases	13
2.4	Petroleum Fiscal Systems	14
2.5	Marginal Fields	22
2.6	Establishment of a Nigerian Limited Liability Company by a Foreign Company	25
THE OIL AND GAS VALUE CHAIN		27
3.1	Upstream: Exploration and Production	28
3.2	Midstream: Transportation and Storage	31
3.3	Downstream: Refining, Petrochemicals and General Industrial Usage	34
CORPORATE GOVERNANCE		37
4.1	Governance Frameworks and Mechanisms	38
4.2	Peer Review	39
HYDROCARBON RESOURCE CLASSIFICATION		43
5.1	Total Petroleum Initially In Place (PIIP)	44
5.2	Discovered Petroleum Initially-In-Place	45
5.3	Undiscovered Petroleum Initially-In-Place	45
5.4	Production	45
5.5	Reserves	45
5.6	Contingent Resources	46
5.7	Prospective Resources	46
5.8	Unrecoverable resources	46
5.9	Estimated Ultimate Recovery (EUR)	47
5.10	Use of Hydrocarbon Resources Terminology	47
5.11	Project Maturation Resource Sub-Classification	48
TERMINOLOGIES IN OIL AND GAS AGREEMENTS		51
THE NIGERIAN-UPSTREAM ENVIRONMENT		65
7.1	Government Agencies	65
7.2	Joint Teams and Interfaces	67
7.3	Roles and Personality	71
7.4	Roles and Networks	72
7.5	Organisational Structure	73
7.6	Leadership Styles	74
7.7	Management Paradoxes	76
7.8	Role Definition Exercise	76
7.9	Management in Teams and Networks	88

SOFT SKILLS FOR THE MANAGER 93
8.1 Inclusive Leadership 95
8.2 How to Lead Yourself 98
8.3 How to Handle Criticism 101

LIST OF FIGURES

FIGURE 1: CLASSIFICATION OF FISCAL SYSTEMS 15
FIGURE 2: ALLOCATION OF REVENUE FROM PRODUCTION (AFTER D. JOHNSTON) 17
FIGURE 3: TYPICAL 'R-FACTOR' DETERMINATION IN NIGERIAN PSCS 19
FIGURE 4: NIGERIAN PSC NOMINAL CONTRACTOR TAKE VALUATION 21
FIGURE 5: MARGINAL FIELD FACTS 24
FIGURE 6: TYPICAL OIL AND GAS VALUE CHAIN COMPONENTS 28
FIGURE 7: UPSTREAM VALUE CHAIN COMPONENTS 29
FIGURE 8: FIVE-YEAR GLOBAL RIG COUNT, OIL PRODUCTION AND PRICE TRENDS 30
FIGURE 9: MIDSTREAM VALUE CHAIN COMPONENTS 32
FIGURE 10: DOWNSTREAM VALUE CHAIN COMPONENTS 34
FIGURE 11: KEY ELEMENTS OF A GOVERNANCE FRAMEWORK (COURTESY DELOITTE) 38
FIGURE 12: PRE-CONCESSION AND E&P ACTIVITIES SHOWING UPSTREAM DECISION GATES 40
FIGURE 13: HYDROCARBON RESOURCE CLASSIFICATION 44
FIGURE 14: RESOURCE SUB-CLASSES BASED ON PROJECT MATURITY 49
FIGURE 15: TYPICAL CONTRACT AREA (COURTESY IHS ENERGY) 54
FIGURE 16: TRADITIONAL EXPLORATION AND PRODUCTION ORGANISATION 69
FIGURE 17: MANAGEMENT INFORMATION FLOW (COURTESY STUDY.COM) 70
FIGURE 18: ORGANISATIONAL SEGMENTS 73
FIGURE 19: COMPETENCY MODEL FOR MANAGERS 75
FIGURE 20: CURRENT ROLE SELF-ANALYSIS 87
FIGURE 21: REVISED ROLE ANALYSIS 88

LIST OF TABLES

TABLE 1: NIGER DELTA PETROLEUM PIPELINE LENGTHS (CIA WORLD FACT BOOK) 35
TABLE 2: GLOSSARY OF TERMS USED IN HYDROCARBON RESOURCE CLASSIFICATION 50
TABLE 3 TASK OVERVIEW OF CURRENT ROLE SELF-ANALYSIS 79
TABLE 4 CURRENT ROLE SELF-ANALYSIS QUESTIONNAIRE 80

An Introduction to Nigerian Upstream Oil and Gas Management

Part One

# CHAPTER ONE
INTRODUCTION

The Oil and Gas segment of the Nigerian economy accounts for some 95% of the export earnings and over 80% of government revenues. Going by the increase in participation by indigenous companies in the provision of services to the Oil and Gas industry, one would have to admit that tremendous progress has been made in building local capacity in the extractive industry.

The flip side of that coin has to do with the quality of the workforce providing the services and, as a direct consequence, the quality of the investment decisions. Project implementation costs are higher than they need to be. This is where the 'role in the middle', the Manager can make a difference in an industry where deliveries are so capital intensive.

The paradox, however, is that the industry has, until recent times, left the commercial and investment decisions in the hands of the 'commercial' folks. This is a paradox because, truth be told, Oil and Gas projects across the entire value chain start and end with the technical valuation and management of hydrocarbon resources. The technical Manager must, of necessity, be an integral part of the critical decision-making processes.

This book will introduce you to Value Chain thinking. To some, this will be a refresher; to others, a paradigm shift. Either way, the intentions of the author would have been fulfilled. But this delivery does not end there. The book is also deliberately designed to introduce the reader to the soft skills required for effective and efficient portfolio management. The curriculum is a rich compendium of lessons learnt over an extended period of time in and out of the industry.

1.1 Facts and Figures

Nigeria is the most populous country within OPEC with around 198 million inhabitants and covers an area of about 924 thousand square kilometres. The country, which joined OPEC in 1971, is located in the Gulf of Guinea on Africa's western coast. The capital is the Federal Capital Territory, Abuja. The official language is English although many local languages such as Hausa, Yoruba, Igbo and Ijaw are also spoken.

Oil was first discovered in Oloibiri, in Nigeria's Bayelsa State, in 1956. Apart from petroleum, Nigeria's other natural resources include natural gas, tin, iron ore, coal, limestone, niobium, lead, zinc and arable land. The oil and gas sector accounts for about 10 per cent of gross domestic product, and petroleum exports revenue accounts for more than 80% of total exports revenue. Its currency is the Nigerian Naira.

Population (million inhabitants)	198
Land/water area ('000 sq. km.)	924
Population density (inhabitants per sq. km.)	214
GDP per capita ($)	1,881
GDP at market prices (million $)	371,886
Value of exports (million $)	46,680
Value of petroleum exports (million $)	,608
Current account balance (million $)	7,924
Proven crude oil reserves (million barrels)	37,453
Proven natural gas reserves (billion cu. m.)	5,627
Crude oil production ('000 b/d)	1,536
Marketed production of natural gas (million cu. m.)	45,434
Refinery capacity ('000 b/cd)	446
Output of petroleum products ('000 b/d)	82
Oil demand ('000 b/d)	426
Crude oil exports ('000 b/d)	1,811
Exports of petroleum products ('000 b/d)	19
Natural gas exports (million cu. m.)	32,511

- b/d-(barrels per day)
- cu. m. (cubic metres)
- b/cd-(barrels per calendar day)

Source: Annual Statistical Bulletin 2018

CHAPTER TWO
NIGERIAN PETROLEUM LEGISLATION   02

2.1 The Department of Petroleum Resources (DPR)

The Department of Petroleum resources (DPR) is the regulatory unit of the Ministry of Petroleum Resources. The unit is vested with the oversight powers of the state for Oil and Gas operations. To this end, the DPR is the custodian of the Petroleum Act (sub-section 2.1.1) and numerous other legislation guiding the conduct of petroleum operations. The DPR supervises the Oil and Gas operations of the state based on these templates.

We shall expatiate on some of the more critical legislation and guidelines in the following sub-sections.

2.1.1 Petroleum Act 1969 Cap 350, Laws of the Federation of Nigeria, 1990

In most countries, including those without production, legislation is enacted to establish sovereignty over natural resources as well as to ensure the proper control and full supervision of the petroleum industry. The ownership and control of all petroleum products is vested in the state in most developing countries. In developed countries where it is not so vested, the state benefits from substantial revenue accruing from petroleum taxes.

In Nigeria, by virtue of the Petroleum Act 1969, the ownership and control of all oil and gas reserves is vested in the state of Nigeria. The Constitution of the Federal Republic of Nigeria 1979 further emphasized the state ownership in section 40 (3).

Ever since the search for oil began in Nigeria, legislation have been passed to control various petroleum activities. The basic legislation is the Petroleum Act 1969 (No. 51) with amendments in 1973, 1976 and 1977. These amendments have been consolidated into the main Act in the revised laws and cited as Petroleum Act 1969 Cap 350, Laws of the Federation of Nigeria, 1990 (the Act).

The Act together with the Petroleum (Drilling and Production) Regulations 1969 (the Regulation) establish the regulatory and administrative framework for the petroleum industry. The Act proclaims Nigeria's national sovereignty over all petroleum reserves, both onshore and offshore.

There are apparent weaknesses in the Act which have continued to be exacerbated and taken advantage of over the years. The Act is no different from most other legislation in this regard. These weaknesses include the vesting of all approval rights in the Minister without provisions for transparency in granting oil licenses and leases. The Act in its present form is also weak on accountability and penalties for offenses are mostly inadequate.

In addition to the Act, the DPR is also guided by numerous additional operational regulations and guidelines, some of which are described in Sub-Sections 2.1.2 to 2.1.4.

2.1.2 Handbook on Petroleum E&P Laws, Regulations & DPR Requirements (2014)

The Handbook is compiled in two parts:
- Part I contains the Acts and related Regulations touching on E&P operations
- Part II treats the types of Approvals, Permits, Guidelines, etc, usually issued or required by the DPR in its role of regulating and guiding E&P operations and activities from the award of blocks (from which marginal fields are excised) to Appraisal, Development, Production and Abandonment of wells.

2.1.3 Guidelines and Procedures for Obtaining Minister's Consent to the Assignment of Interest in Oil and Gas Assets (2014)

These Guidelines are issued pursuant to the provisions of paragraphs 14-16 of the First Schedule to the Petroleum Act, CAP P10 LFN, 2004 and section 17 (5) (d) of the Oil Pipelines Act, CAP O7 LFN 2004.

The purpose of these guidelines is to establish the procedure for obtaining the consent of the Minister of Petroleum Resources to any assignment of any right, power or interest in an Oil Prospecting Licence (OPL), Oil Mining Lease (OML), Marginal Field (MF) or Oil and Gas Pipelines Licence (OGPL) in accordance with the Petroleum Act and the Oil Pipelines Act.

2.1.4 Guidelines for Farm-Out and Operation of Marginal Fields in Nigeria (2010)

These Guidelines have been prepared pursuant to the provisions of Paragraph 16A of the first Schedule to the Petroleum Act CAP P10 LFN 2004.

A Marginal Field (MF) is defined as any field that has reserves booked and reported annually to the Department of Petroleum Resources (DPR) and has remained unproduced for a period of not less than 10 years from the date of discovery of the field.

2.2 The Petroleum Industry Bill

A major review of existing legislation is ongoing. It has given birth to the Nigerian Petroleum Industry Governance Bill (PIGB) which is yet to be fully passed into law. The Bill was originally proposed as a single document to cover all aspects of the Oil and Gas value chain and was referred to in a general sense as the Petroleum Industry Bill (PIB). However, the complexities of the Nigerian geopolitical environment precluded the passage of such an omnibus piece of legislation into law.

The PIGB was passed by both the Senate and House of Representatives in March 2018. This first harmonised draft of the PIGB was transmitted by the National Assembly to the President for assent into law on June 8, 2018. This milestone was attained 17 years after commencement of efforts to update the legal framework of Nigeria's Oil and Gas industry. The objectives of the PIGB are to:

1. Create efficient and effective governing institutions with clear and separate roles for the petroleum industry;
2. Establish a framework for the creation of commercially oriented and profit driven petroleum entities to ensure value addition and internationalisation of the petroleum industry;
3. Promote transparency and accountability in the administration of petroleum resources of Nigeria; and
4. Foster a conducive business environment for petroleum industry operations.

The PIGB in its current form is that portion of the "original" comprehensive PIB which deals with the regulatory aspects and has been renamed appropriately. Its passage into law however remains elusive.

The remaining Bills include the Petroleum Industry Administration Bill (PIAB), Petroleum Industry Fiscal Bill (PIFB), and the Petroleum Host Communities Bill (PHCB), which complement the Petroleum Industry Governance Bill (PIGB) to ensure holistic reform of the petroleum industry.

When fully passed along with the fiscal and social responsibility/community components, it is expected to replace the Act in its entirety. The Act subsists until date pending the full enactment of the PIGB and its ancillary components.

2.3 Licenses and Leases

Schedule I to the Act stipulates the terms of Oil Exploration Licenses (OEL), Oil Prospecting Licenses (OPL), and Oil Mining Leases (OML), and the 1969 Regulations stipulates their conditions. The format of an OEL, OPL and OML as well as the format for the respective applications are set out in the schedule to the Regulations.

2.3.1 *Oil Exploration License (OEL)*

This is a non-exclusive license for the licensee to explore for petroleum by surface geological and geophysical methods for a limited period. It does not confer any right to the grant of an OPL or an OML. The regulation size of an OEL is 12,950 sq.km.

2.3.2 *Oil Prospecting License (OPL)*

This confers exclusive rights of surface and subsurface exploration for petroleum in an area not more than 2,590 sq.km. in size for an initial period of five (5) years for onshore and inland basins and 10 years for offshore and deep offshore blocks.

The holder of an OPL may carry away and dispose of petroleum discovered during prospecting operations, subject to the fulfilment of obligations imposed by or under the law, including any special terms or conditions imposed by the Minister of Petroleum Resources such as government participation in the venture and any special provision relating to any natural gas discovered (Schedule 1, Para 34 of the Act).

2.3.3 Oil Mining Lease (OML)

This grants exclusive rights to explore, discover, produce, transport and carry away petroleum from the leased area subject to the Petroleum Act 1969 and any special terms and conditions imposed under schedule 1 paragraph 34 of the Act. The maximum size of an OML as stipulated in the Regulations is 1,295 sq.km and the specified duration is 20 years. This period may however be renewed in accordance with the Act by the holder of an OML.

The Operator of an OPL or OML is obliged under the law to relinquish a contiguous area totalling 50% of the contract area upon application for either a conversion from OPL to OML or an extension of the OML period. Ownership of the relinquished area shall revert to government which retains the right to award the acreage to any potential investor through a competitive bid-round.

2.4 Petroleum Fiscal Systems

A Petroleum Fiscal System (PFS) is a description of the legislative, tax, contractual and fiscal elements under which petroleum operations are conducted in a petroleum province, region or area. It defines the relationship between mineral owners (host government) and the Oil and Gas companies. The PFS is crucial to an equitable determination of how costs are recovered and profits are shared among the stakeholders (firms, host governments and mineral owners).

Usually, the host government (HG) wants to retain as much profit as possible through levies, taxes, royalty and bonuses. The various

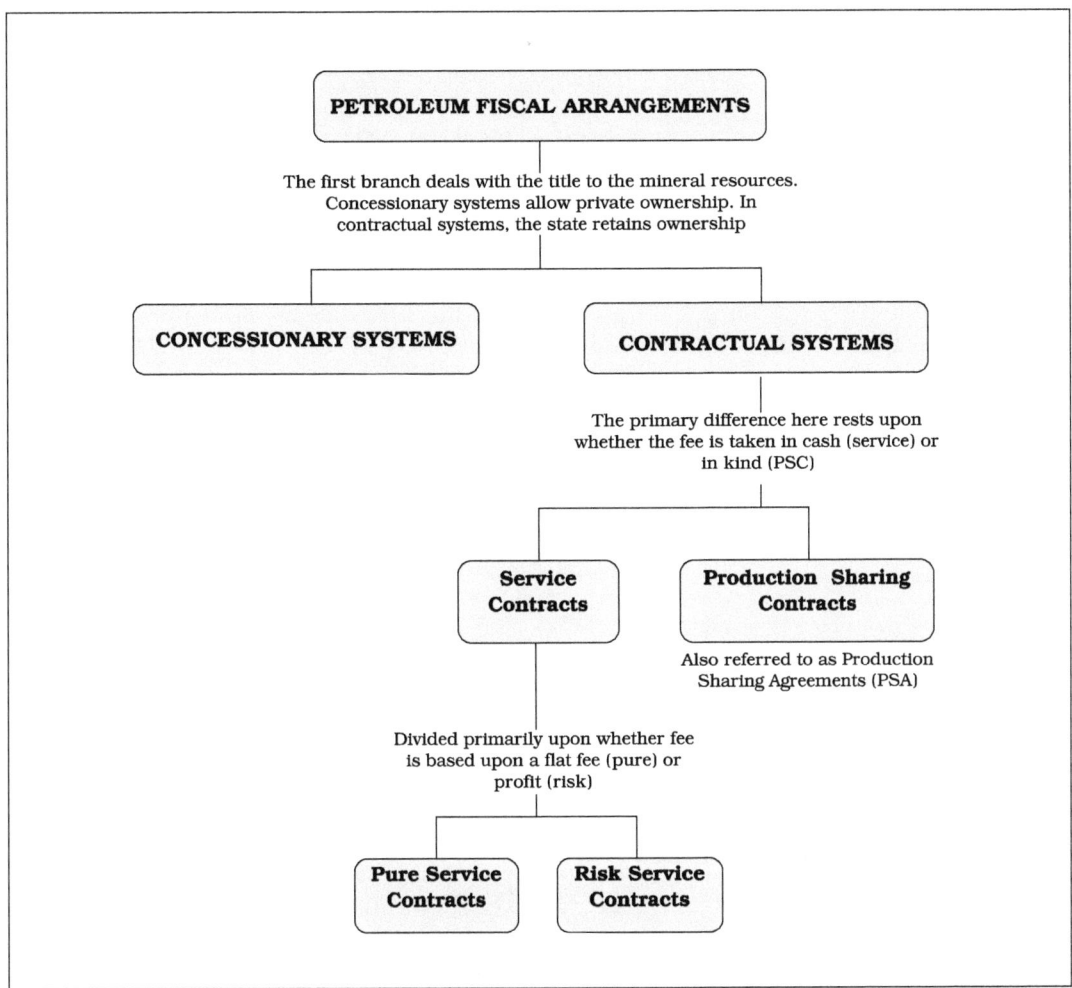

Figure - 1: Classification of Fiscal Systems

The philosophical difference between the Service Contracts (SC) and Production Sharing Contracts (PSC) is the method of payment for services, either by cash (SC) or in kind (PSC). Service Contracts are further divided into two depending on whether the service fee is a flat fee (pure) or profit share (risk).

Because there are only subtle differences between SCs and PSCs, the study of PSCs effectively covers the entire contractual branch of the tree. Much of the language and commercial attributes of PSCs and service agreements are identical. The differences, especially from a practical and financial point of view, are mostly semantic. This book concentrates on terminology. The economic valuations are better covered in a Petroleum Economics course.

2.4.1 Production Sharing Contracts

This sub-section elaborates on some of the key attributes of PSCs in the Nigerian Oil and Gas operating environment. Under the PSCs, the Nigerian National Petroleum Corporation (NNPC) is the holder of the concession (Concessionaire) on behalf of the state. The Operator and its partners, if applicable, is defined as the Contractor or Contractor Group as the case may be. This family of agreements outnumber service contracts 5 to 1 globally and the Nigerian government has elected to use the PSC template for all licences going forward. The upstream Manager must, therefore, develop a familiarity with its attributes.

The first thing to note about a PSC is that it is a contractor-funded risk contract with a profit share component. PSCs were a novelty when first introduced in 1990 with the Ashland Oil agreements. The concept became widely accepted in 1993 as an improvement on the deficient Joint Venture arrangements. Eight (8) contracts were executed in 1993, attracting foreign investment because of their favourable fiscal and legal regimes. The Operator was granted a larger profit share for the more marginal and higher risk projects offshore.

A second batch of eight (8) PSCs were signed in 2000 as a consequence of Nigeria's foray into the deep-water frontier. The profit-sharing terms, predicated on reduced risks involved in finding larger deep-water reserves, were however considered less favourable for the oil companies. The learnings from the 1993 and 2000 rounds were brought to bear in 2005 when 14 deep-water licenses were offered. One can thus adduce that the Nigerian PSC regime has come to stay.

The contractor, under this scheme, bears the costs and risks of exploration and development activities to first oil. A built-in cost recovery mechanism allows the contractor to recover a negotiated percentage of all agreed costs on a year-on-year basis in production until full cost recovery. The remaining production is shared based on an agreed profit oil split and taxes are levied on the contractor's overall profit as shown in Figure 2. The succeeding sub-sections highlight the main attributes of a PSC.

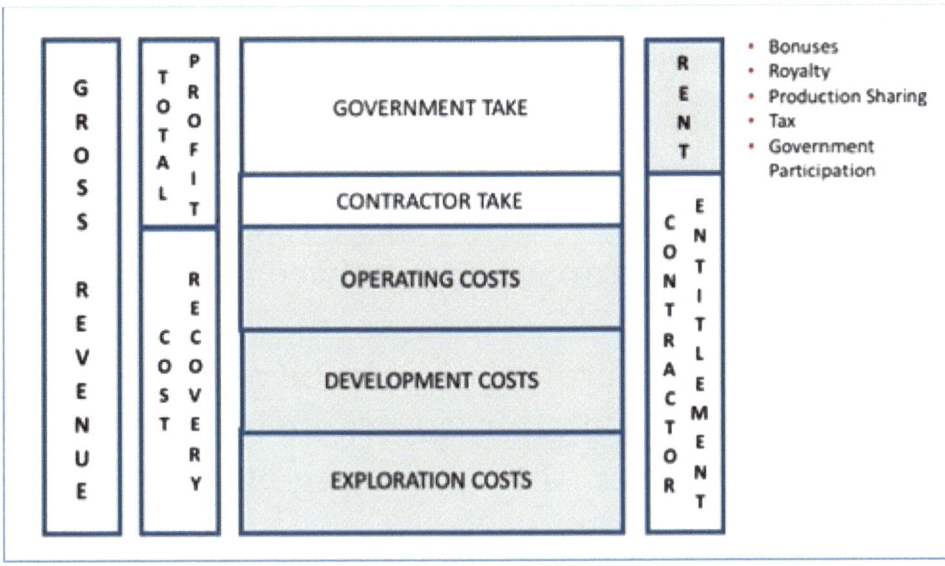

Figure - 2: *Allocation of Revenue from Production (After D. Johnston)*

2.4.1.1 Bonuses

The Nigerian PSCs contain both signature and production bonuses. These are fixed fees which are paid by the Operator to the Federal Government at different stages of the project. Signature bonuses are paid immediately after the completion of negotiations and signing of the PSC while production bonuses are paid when the production from a specific contract area reaches a particular threshold. Bonus payments do not qualify for cost recovery.

2.4.1.2 Royalty

Royalty is a quarterly levy applied to gross production. These payments are determined based on gross production and allocated to NNPC for payment on behalf of itself and the Operator as per the schedule in the Petroleum Act. Royalty always comes first in the hierarchy of deductions.

The only exemptions are deep-water contract areas with water depths in excess of 1000 metres where royalty is not applicable.

2.4.1.3   Cost Recovery

After royalty oil is backed out, cost oil is allocated to the Operator to recover all its operating costs. Operating expenses incurred on different Oil Prospecting Licences are ring-fenced with or without a negotiated maximum cost recovery limit (cap). Cross ring fence transactions within a single company are treated as transactions between associates.

The PSC usually provides for operating costs to be recovered in the year of expenditure while capital costs are recoverable in equal instalments over a five-year period or over the remaining life of the contract, whichever is less.

2.4.1.4   Tax

The next tranche of deductions is for taxation and is allocated to the NNPC for payment on behalf of itself and the Operator. The difference between the proceeds and deductible costs of the entire project is taxable under the Petroleum Profits Tax Act, LFN 1990 (PPTA).

2.4.1.5   Profit Oil

This is an important component of the business for all stakeholders. We will take some time to explain the exotic production based sliding scale used in its determination in the Nigerian PSCs.

Once the allocation of royalty oil, cost oil and tax oil has been made, the remaining oil is shared between the NNPC and the contractor in accordance with a previously agreed profit split based on cumulative levels of production. Rather than set the share ratios as fixed percentages for the lifetime of the PSA or as a progressive (upwardly increasing) scale designed to increase the state's participation levels as the underlying project attains greater levels of daily production, the Nigerian PSCs create a sliding scale of profit shares using what is popularly known as an "R-Factor" (or Ratio Factor). The R-Factor is derived by dividing the revenues from a project by the costs of that project as presented in Figure 3.

R Factor	CONTRACTOR Share	CORP. Share
R < 1.2	P = 70%	100% - P
1.2 < R < 2.5	P = 25%+[(2.5-R)/(2.5-1.2)*(70%-25%)]	100% - P
R > 2.5	P = 25%	100% - P

Where, for each Contract Area:

$R^n = ((PO^1 + CO^1) * RP^1 + (PO^2 + CO^2) * RP^2 + \ldots + (PO^{n-1} + CO^{n-1}) * RP^{n-1}) /$ (Cumulative capital + cumulative non-capital costs)

Where
PO=Contractor share of profit oil
CO=Cost oil
RP=Realizable price
n= The actual accounting period

Figure - 3: Typical 'R-Factor' Determination in Nigerian PSCs

At the start of the project, costs inevitably outweigh revenues and so the R-Factor will be zero or low. As the R-Factor increases with growing revenues in the later stages of the project, the profit share increases in favour of the state. In other words, as the net profitability of the Operator increases, its profit share reduces. This is designed to maintain the equilibrium of the original agreement.

2.4.1.6 Term and Relinquishment

The PSC terms span a period of approximately 30 years comprising 10 years of exploration (as OPL; Section 2.3.2) and 20 years of development and production (as OML; Section 2.3.3) with a provision for relinquishment of as much as 50% of the initial contract area upon conversion from OPL to OML.

2.4.1.7 Management Committee

The PSC provides for a management committee which is similar to the operating committee under a joint venture. The committee consists of members of both the NNPC and the contractor group. The NNPC (represented by NAPIMS) is tasked with the management of the operation while the operating company is responsible for the execution of the approved work programme.

2.4.1.8 Minimum Work Program

The contractor is obliged to execute a minimum work program during the OPL phase. This is usually specified as 3D seismic coverage and number of wells. This commitment is a critical part of the PSC and is, therefore, required to be backed up with a Performance Bond from a reputable and approved financial institution. The Operator provides the necessary funds for the execution of the work programme.

2.4.1.9 National Interest Provisions

The Nigerian PSC contains clauses which protect Nigeria's national economic interests by providing for technology transfer, training of local employees and preference for local suppliers as is required by the Local Content Act and Petroleum Act.

2.4.2 PSC Valuation

As a rule of thumb, proved-developed-producing (PDP) reserves (see Chapter 5 for resource classification) are worth 0.5 to 0.7 of the wellhead price multiplied by the contractor's take. This rule should only be used to estimate the present value of the contractor's working-interest share of proved-developed-producing reserves assuming there are no major sunk costs eligible for recovery.

Conversely, the value of undeveloped reserves is usually less than 50% the value of PDP reserves. A nominal contractor's take valuation flow is shown in Figure 4.

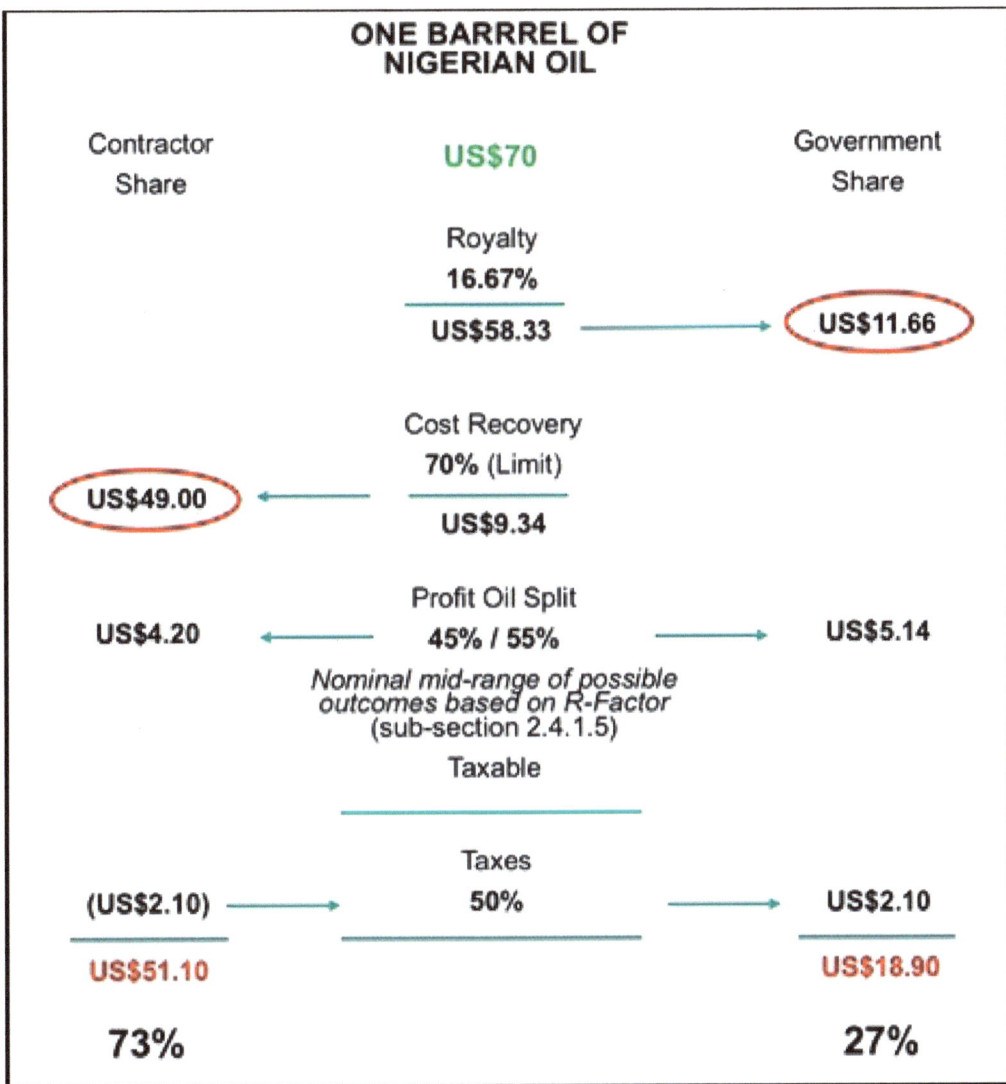

Figure - 4: Nigerian PSC Nominal Contractor Take Valuation

2.4.3 Other Agreements

In addition to the two main types of contractual systems of agreements (the SC and the PSC), there are two other arrangements that are often utilised in the Nigerian Oil and Gas industry which pre-date the PSCs.

They are:

1. Joint ventures
2. Technical Service Agreements, Enhanced Oil Recovery (EOR) contracts

Joint ventures (JVs) are not a type of fiscal/contractual system. They are made popular in the industry through standard joint operating agreements (JOAs) and working interest arrangements between companies. The term is primarily used to describe arrangements where the national oil company is in partnership with the contractor. Thus, governments get directly involved through joint ventures.

Technical Service Agreements (TSAs) are used for Enhanced Oil recovery (EOR) projects or rehabilitation/redevelopment schemes administered under a PSC or a concessionary system. These normally involve proved reserves that are beyond the primary recovery stage. This creates quite a different setting from normal exploration and development economics. The critical aspect of exploration risk is missing.

2.5 Marginal Fields

From an economic perspective, there are good fields with no serious questions about development decisions. There are also 'bad' fields, the type for which development options are deferred for a few years or dropped altogether, pending technological advancement. Beyond these, there are marginal fields.

In Nigeria, the Marginal Fields initiative is a key deliverable of the national strategic goals to meet production targets of 4 million barrels/day and 40 billion barrels of oil reserves by 2020.

Any un-produced field that has an exploratory well drilled on the structure and had been reported as an oil and/or gas discovery for a period of not less than 10 years from the date of discovery, or any field that the present leaseholders may consider for farm-out due to portfolio rationalisation is classified as a Marginal Field (MF).

The Nigerian Marginal Field program is a strategic initiative designed to achieve the following:

1. Expand the scope of participation in Nigeria's oil industry and diversify the sources of investment and the inflow of funds
2. Increase the oil and gas reserves base through aggressive exploration
3. Promote indigenous participation in the oil industry thereby fostering technology transfer
4. Provide an opportunity for portfolio rationalisation.
5. Provide an opportunity to gainfully engage the pool of high level technically competent Nigerians in the oil and gas business
6. Promote common usage of assets/facilities to ensure optimum utilisation of available excess capacities
7. Expand production output capacity
8. Enhance employment opportunity

In the period since formal implementation in 2001, the Nigerian MF program has yielded the results shown in Figure 5.

> - The first marginal field to be farmed out, following the passage of the Act, was the Ogbelle Field
>   - farmed out by Chevron Nigeria Limited in 1997.
> - The first bid round to be formally organized started in 2001, and was concluded in 2003
>   - 24 licenses were awarded to 31 indigenous companies.
> - A second round of awards was proposed for 2013 under similar guidelines but was later aborted.
> - In total, 30 Marginal Field Licenses have been awarded since the policy was introduced in Nigeria.
> - Of the current licensees, some 30% of the fields have attained commercial production.
> - Marginal field production made up some 3% of crude oil output between 2015 and 2016.

Figure - 5: Marginal Field Facts

Experience has revealed that the oil price cycle is not relevant to most Marginal projects. The economic life is too short. As a general rule therefore, if the available price is not good enough; be patient. Put the project on the shelf and wait. The reality is that the price of oil cannot be guaranteed. Similarly, reserves are not guaranteed. From an economic perspective, we can lock in the price on the futures market but we cannot lock in the reserves.

We could summarise the rules of engagement for Marginal Fields as follows:

- Think portfolio rather than single accumulation acquisitions
- Spread the risk across the portfolio and thus improve the probability of success
- Do not be ruled by oil price uncertainty; defer implementation if you must
- Be patient and mitigate low oil price risk by locking in (high) when possible
- Do not attempt to kill a fly with a sledgehammer: do not overwork the problem

2.6 Establishment of a Nigerian Limited Liability Company by a Foreign Company

One vital input to the realisation of the overall national objectives of the MF program is the partnership between indigenous and foreign companies. This requires the establishment of local affiliates by the foreign oil companies. For seamless relationships between local and foreign entities, it is of vital importance to be familiar with the legal prerequisites. We shall enumerate a few of these in the following sub-sections.

2.6.1 Legal Entity

Nigerian company law requires the incorporation of a Nigerian company if a foreign person or company wishes to engage in business activities in Nigeria or hold landed property in Nigeria.

Unlike other jurisdictions of the world where representative or branch offices of foreign companies may operate without being incorporated, foreign companies must be registered in Nigeria as limited liability companies.

2.6.2 Incorporation

Foreign company incorporation is under the purview of the Corporate Affairs Commission (CAC). A Certificate of Incorporation containing the company's registration number is issued at the conclusion of the process.

The company must have at least two directors and two shareholders who may be individuals or corporate entities. It is not necessary for the directors to be Nigerian citizens. Where a company is incorporated with foreign shareholders, it will need to complete registration with the Nigerian Investment Promotion Commission (NIPC) before it commences business.

The company's Memorandum and Articles of Association must contain the key objects or purposes for which the company is being established.

2.6.3 Incorporation Requirements

In summary, the requirements for foreign company domiciliation in Nigeria include, but may not be limited to:

a) Incorporation (name search, reservation and registration)
b) Income and Value Added Tax registrations
c) Application for Business Permit
d) Application for Expatriate quota positions
e) Certificate of Capital Importation
f) Immigration formalities – Residence Permit

The entity may begin operations after the name search and incorporation process have been completed. This takes approximately four (4) weeks from commencement of the process. A total of three (3) to four (4) months is required to complete the entire process of incorporation.

It is recommended that a firm of competent lawyers be engaged to handle this aspect.

CHAPTER THREE

THE OIL AND GAS VALUE CHAIN   03

The Oil and Gas industry encompasses a range of activities and processes which jointly contribute to the transformation of underground petroleum resources into useable end-products valued by industrial and private customers. These different activities are inherently linked to each other (conceptually, contractually and/or physically) and these linkages might occur within or across individual firms, and within or across national boundaries.

For the purposes of this book, value creation is seen as a benefit to respective companies, of which different aspects are captured by different professionals. The value chain analysis, as popularised by Porter (1985), investigates the sequence of consecutive activities which are required to bring a product or service from conception and procurement, through the different phases of production and distribution, to the final customer. For Oil and Gas, the principal stages are the discovery, evaluation, development, production, processing, transportation and marketing of hydrocarbons.

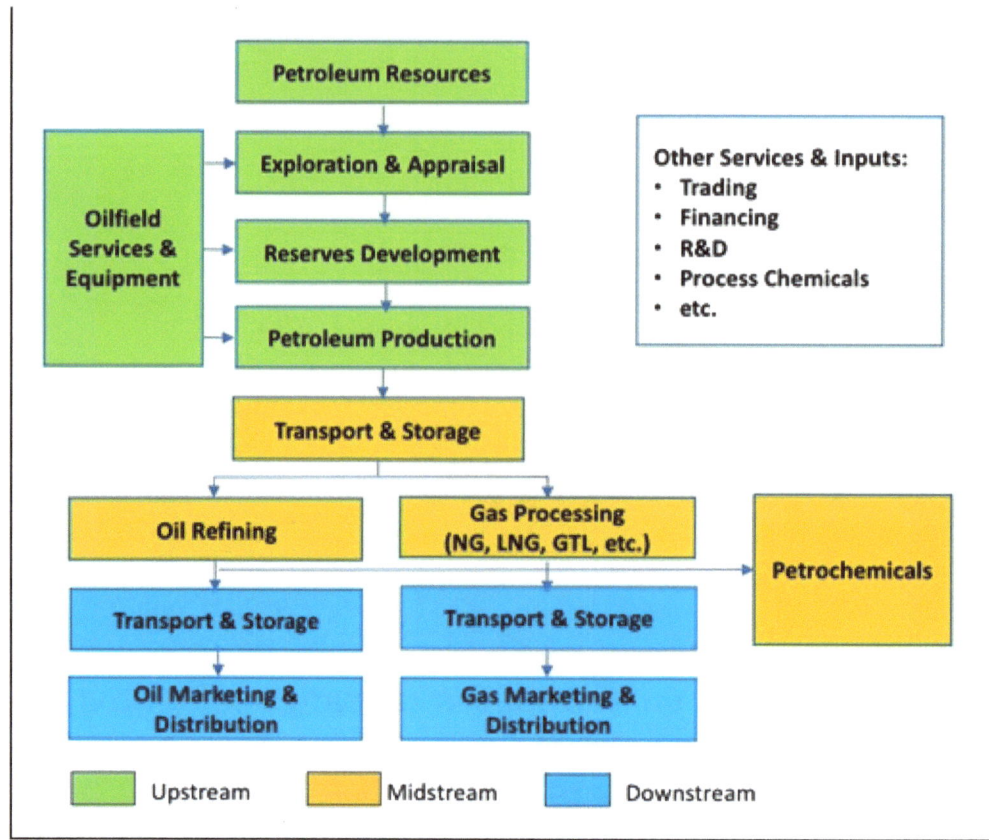

Figure 6: Typical Oil and Gas Value Chain Components

The focus of this book is to understand value creation at company level rather than private shareholder value (macro versus micro). We shall briefly describe the key activities of the petroleum sector. Some aspects of the different stages of the value chain will also be presented. Although all stages of the industry value chain will be discussed, there is a deliberate emphasis on upstream operations. Overall, this section seeks to introduce the big picture, value drivers and risk factors of the petroleum industry. It does not seek to address the rudiments of the various professional and cross functional aspects which are covered adequately in other specialised publications.

3.1 Upstream: Exploration and Production

The identification of suitable sedimentary basins for oil and/or gas exploration is usually done using relatively simple means such as aerial and satellite photography, as well as aeromagnetic surveys. Detailed information of a smaller area is then obtained through dedicated seismic surveys, which are considerably higher resolution and more expensive. Through an integrated process of data acquisition, processing and interpretation, the data is transformed into an image of the subsurface and possible indications of hydrocarbon deposits.

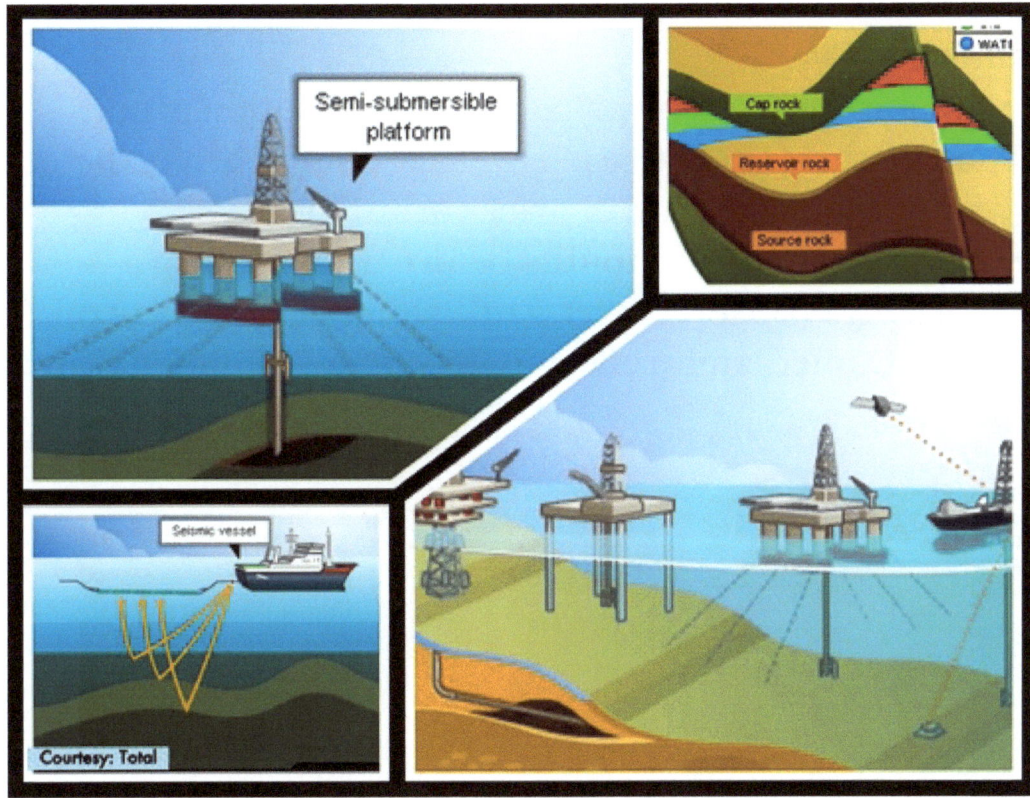

Figure 7: Upstream Value Chain Components

Exploratory drilling is the next step after creating an image of the subsurface and evaluating the commercial viability of the possible hydrocarbon accumulations. This involves the contracting and deployment of drilling rigs suitable for the respective environments (i.e. land, swamp, shallow water or deep-water). There are considerable ancillary equipment, products and services associated with drilling, and many petroleum companies typically contract service companies for these tasks.

The market for drill rigs and drilling services is considered a reliable lead indicator for the overall activity and investment level in the industry.

Khalifa, Caporin and Hammoudeh in their paper "The relationship between oil prices and rig counts: The importance of lags" make three (3) important observations:

1. Increase in oil revenues positively affect rig counts. This is confirmed by the five-year oil price and global rig deployment trend (shown in Figure 8).
2. The relationship between oil price and rig utilisation is non-linear. The quantum of change in rig usage cannot be predicted by a corresponding quantum in price variation.
3. There is a lag of up to three months before the impact of a change in pricing is observed in rig utilisation. Changes in oil prices are not immediately reflected in changes in the rig count.

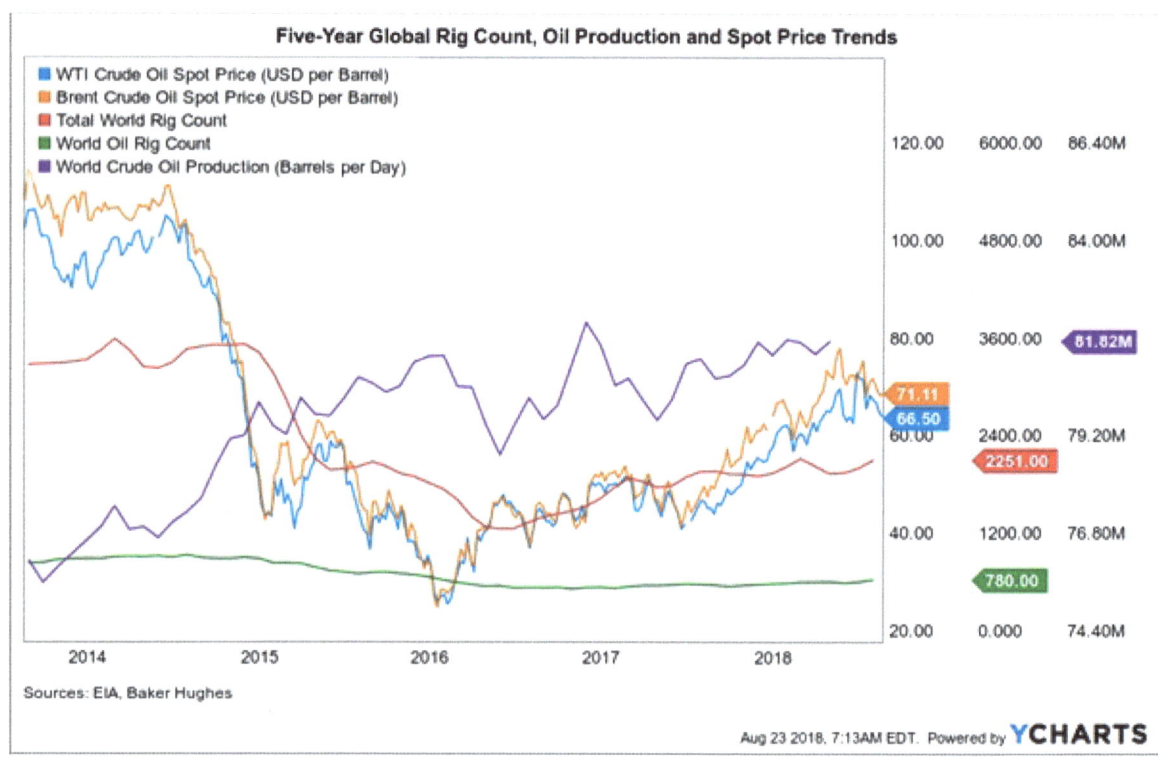

Figure - 8: Five-Year Global Rig Count, Oil Production and Price Trends

The models show that the impact of oil revenues, positive or negative, on changes in rig counts becomes stronger when revenues take a large dip. Notice, therefore, that the effect of the 70% plunge in pricing from mid-2014 was predictable. In this scenario, an ensuing large fall in rig count

With the exception of the floaters, the onshore installations (including the flow stations and integrated tank farms) are connected by some 12,414 km of pipelines of various sizes, making Nigeria's pipeline network the 28th largest amongst the world's 98 Oil and Gas producers. Table 1 breaks down the pipeline lengths.

Classification	Total Pipeline Length (km)
Condensate	124
Gas	4,045
LPG	164
Oil	4,441
Refined	3,640

Table 1: Niger Delta Petroleum Pipeline Lengths (CIA World Fact book)

Refined products from Kaduna, Warri and Port-Harcourt refineries as well as approved mini-refineries and topping plants are distributed by the same means as crude oil. Road transport is probably the most common, but there also exists an extensive network of product pipelines within the country.

The transport options for gas depend on its physical state. Natural gas liquids are transported either by pipeline or tanker truck. Beyond domestic consumption for industrial usage and power generation, long distance gas export from Nigeria is in the form of liquefied natural gas (LNG) from Bonny Terminal. Feedstock for the six (6) trains of the Nigeria LNG plant is delivered via the Offshore Gas Gathering System (OGGS) operated by Shell on behalf of NNPC and other stakeholders.

The Niger Delta basin is known to contain up to 200 trillion cu. ft. of gas resources. However, the enabling major plant/pipeline projects require substantial upfront investment, and would not be viable without clearly identifiable and long-term committed users, a sound revenue/tariff model and tailored financing. When more than one country is involved as is the case with Nigeria, such projects are further subjected to geopolitical considerations.

3.3 Downstream: Refining, Petrochemicals and General Industrial Usage

Detailed treatment of the downstream Oil and Gas business is beyond the scope of this workbook. We, however, offer the comments in this section for completeness.

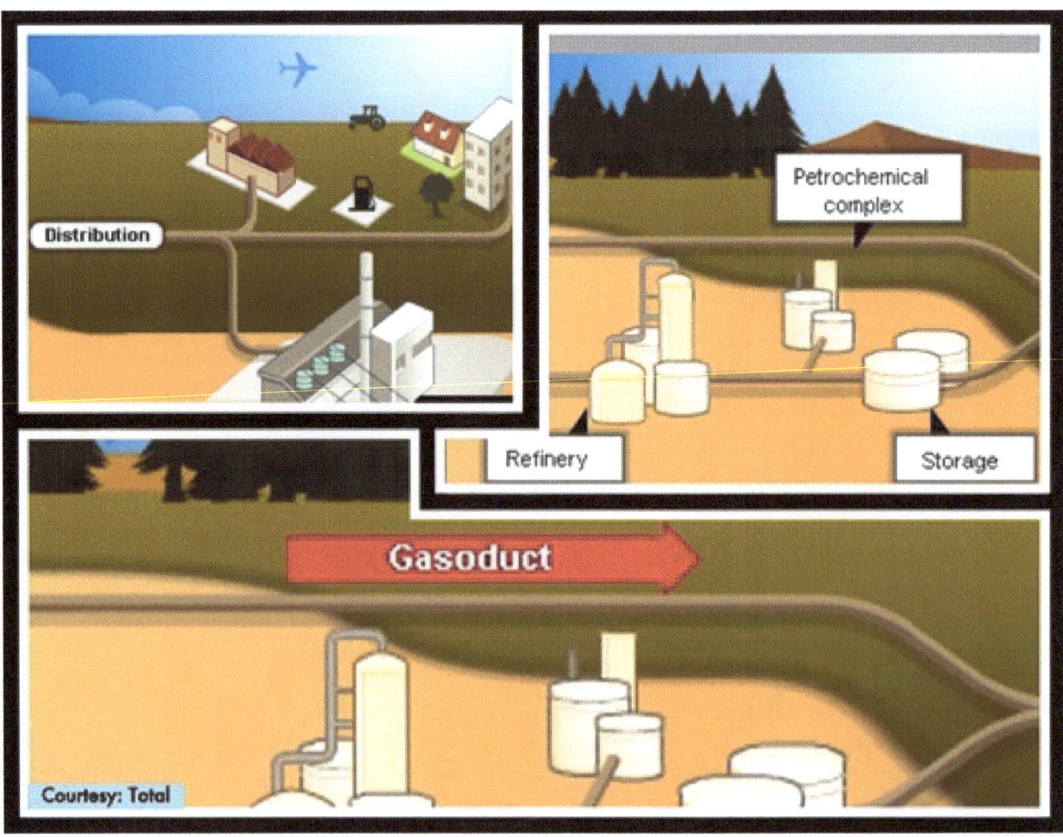

Figure - 10: Downstream Value Chain Components

Crude oil almost always needs to be refined into its different components prior to consumption. The refined products include fuel oil, gas oil, jet fuel/kerosene, gasoline, naphtha and liquefied petroleum gas (LPG). In-country installed crude oil refining capacity is estimated at 445,000 barrels per day from four (4) refineries, two in Port Harcourt, and one each in Kaduna and Warri.

Gas, on the other hand, also requires fractionation to separate the Natural Gas Liquids (NGLs) from the dry gas. NGLs are further fractionated into their constituent parts and sold. In addition to piped natural gas and NGLs, Liquefied Natural Gas (LNG) and Gas-to-Liquids (GTL) are also core marketable products of gas processing.

Petrochemicals are chemicals made from crude oil and natural gas. The two main groups of petrochemicals are olefins and aromatics. Chemical products derived from these are the basis for the manufacture of everyday products such as PVC pipes, plastic bags, bottles, electronic components, car tires and many other products.

Because of the advantages of proximity to process optimisation, refineries and petrochemical plants are often situated next to each other. They also have pipeline linkages between them. The Nigerian National Petroleum Corporation (NNPC) produces linear alkyl benzene, benzene, heavy alkylate and deparaffinised kerosene at its Kaduna Refinery complex. Linked to the Warri Refinery are a 35,000 metric ton per annum (mtpa) polypropylene plant and an 18,000 mtpa carbon black plant.

Marketing, the downstream end member of the value chain, ties it all together. In general terms, it refers to the distribution and sale of refined products, whether wholesale or retail in petrol stations.

CHAPTER FOUR

CORPORATE GOVERNANCE   04

> *It is not the mistake that causes the serious damage.*
> *It is the mistake that you make of defending the*
> *first mistake that causes it.*
> *- Albert Einstein*

According to the Organisation for Co-operation and Development (OECD, 2004) corporate governance refers to the relationships between a company's management, its board, shareholders, and other stakeholders. It provides the structure through which the objectives of the company are set. It describes the means of attaining those objectives and performance monitoring. Corporate governance is therefore an organic process.

In the introductory section of this book, the point was made that tremendous progress has been recorded in building local capacity in the Nigerian Oil and Gas industry. However, the quality of the workforce providing the services as well as the quality of the completion milestone and investment decisions are sometimes questionable. Project implementation costs are often higher than necessary. It takes only a few capital-intensive project failures to do irreparable damage to corporate assurance, reliability of project reporting, tools and techniques.

The Manager's role is to ensure a positive impact on process enhancements, cost control and quality assurance. If more people are involved in the governance process and how different elements of a governance system interact, there will be significant improvement in project governance.

4.1 Governance Frameworks and Mechanisms

Sources of funding and investment must be convinced that there are adequate controls, checks and balances within a governance framework. Additionally, the view of earnings and balance sheet performance can be impaired by the lack of trust and confidence in the numbers that are published without proper oversight. Internally, the lack of governance can lead to inefficiencies in the system in areas such as capital deployment, organisational performance and operational issues.

The attributes of a typical good governance system are shown in Figure 11.

Governance Framework			
Value	**Operating Model**	**Management System**	**Governing Bodies**
A defined set of values that resonate with the business and are: • Clear; • Memorable; • Mission focused; and • Guide decision-making The values naturally extend to the behaviours expected of individual employees and become guiding principles for "doing things right".	An explanation of: • The distinction between an operational role and a function role; • Delegations; and • How the business plans its activities plus measures its success against that plan	Documented: • Policies, procedures and guidance-ordered in a hierarchy; • Process of self-attestation; and • Summary of how the business operates	Roles and responsibilities at a 'corporate' level e.g.: • Charters of the Board and its sub committees; • Non executive and top tier executive roles and responsibilities; • The role of Internal Audit (IA), compliance and risk management: and • The role of bodies such as a Functional Council to control and maintain policies and procedures etc.

Figure - 11: Key Elements of a Governance Framework (courtesy Deloitte)

Since governance mechanisms can be split into two categories, internal and external, it is important to differentiate between both. Each category deploys different sets of governance mechanisms and the authority for their management belong to different groups.

Charlie Weir, David Laing and Phillip J. McKnight in their paper titled Internal and External Governance Mechanisms: Their Impact on the Performance of Large UK Public Companies surmise that the external governance framework sets standards, actions, and other requirements that society expects a company to follow. In other words, the external governance framework seeks to produce standards of behaviour and actions externally and between organisations.

Our focus in this book is on internal governance. This is a set of mechanisms and processes that are used to organise, coordinate and govern internally. In other words, internal governance seeks to guide actions and produce standards for use within an organisation.

4.2 Peer Review

Peer review is the cross-disciplinary evaluation of work by functional project teams/task forces of similar competence to the producers of the work (peers). It constitutes a form of self-regulation by qualified professionals within the relevant disciplines. Peer review methods are employed to maintain standards of quality, improve performance, and provide credibility. A peer review is categorized by the type of activity and by the field or profession in which the activity occurs. For example, in the academia, scholarly peer review is often used to determine an academic paper's suitability for publication.

The use of Peer Groups in the assurance process is quite popular in the Oil and Gas industry. To make this work, a complementary Decision Gate template is implemented as part of the Management System shown in Figure 11 in the preceding Section 4.1. The Peer Group functions as the Governing Body. This is the quality assurance team and usually comprises a broad spectrum of disciplines and subject matter experts at the Functional Chiefs/Consultant level. These are typically organised across disciplines and underpinned by project stage/maturity as shown in Figure 12.

As shown in the figure, there are typically four (4) phases in the upstream segment of the Oil and Gas value chain. They are depicted as Phases 1 to 4. The interface between any two phases is what is generally known as a Decision Gate. The terminology may vary from one company to another but the intention remains the same: quality assurance with particular emphasis on corporate governance.

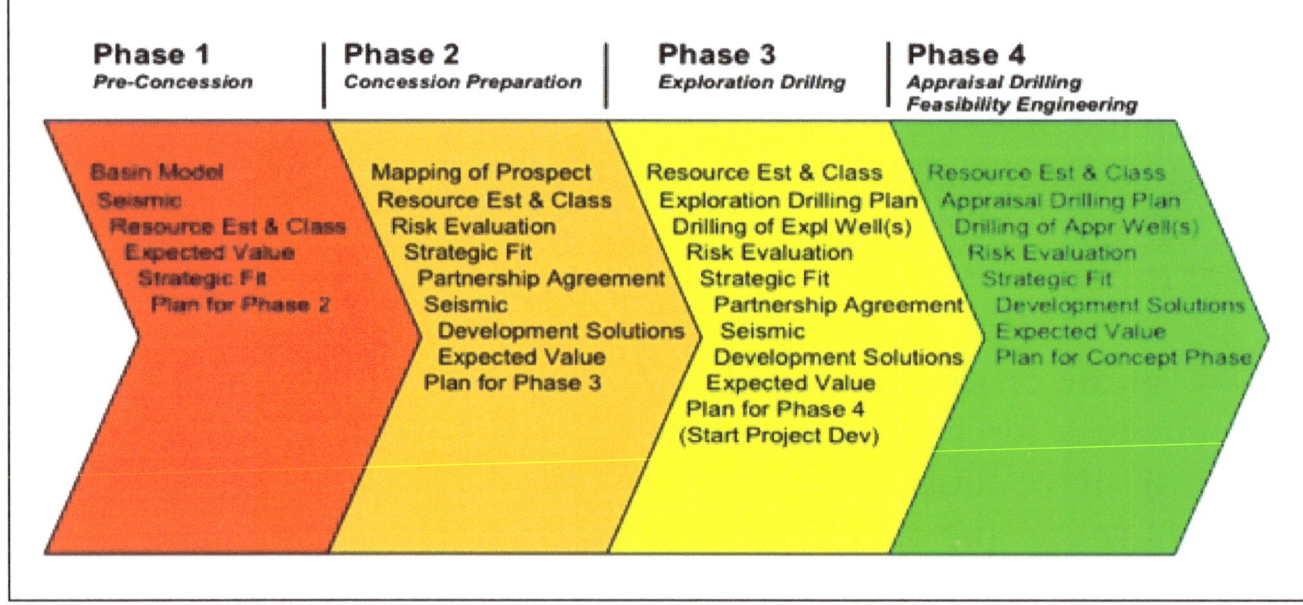

Figure - 12: Pre-Concession and E&P Activities Showing Upstream Decision Gates

A Decision Gate remains closed and further investment decisions are withheld until the agreed criteria to progress are met by the project team. Typical qualification checklists for each phase are as stated in the figure. It is to be noted that these are minimum requirements and these have to be met both in quantum and quality.

For example, a new exploration asset acquisition would be classified at the onset as "Phase 1 Pre-Concession" activity. The listed Decision Gate elements (Basin Model, Seismic, Resource Estimates/Classification, Expected Value, Strategic Fit, Plan for Phase 2) must be in place and up to corporate standards. These are minimum requirements for corporate approval to proceed with the acquisition and move to Phase 2. A similar process is deployed for Phases 2, 3 and 4 Decision Gate activities.

The Peer Groups (Governing Body: broad spectrum of disciplines and subject matter experts at the Functional Chiefs/Consultant level) take ownership of the assurance process and ratify decisions to either proceed to the next stage or defer until more work is carried out. On rare occasions, the decision could be to suspend or terminate a project based on commercial considerations and agreed corporate metrics.

CHAPTER FIVE
HYDROCARBON RESOURCE CLASSIFICATION   05

This part of the book deals with the classification of hydrocarbon resources. This is perhaps the single, most rigorous input to upstream project valuation. It is the primary input into Financial Investment Decisions (FID), a multidisciplinary commercialisation process.

It is generally agreed and approved to use the Society of Petroleum Engineers (SPE) Petroleum Resources Management System (PRMS) as the basis for hydrocarbon resource classification globally.

The term 'resources' refers to all quantities of petroleum naturally occurring on or within the earth's crust, discovered and undiscovered (recoverable and unrecoverable), plus those quantities already produced. The term includes all types of petroleum whether currently considered 'conventional' or 'unconventional.

The SPE classification template is shown in Figure 13.

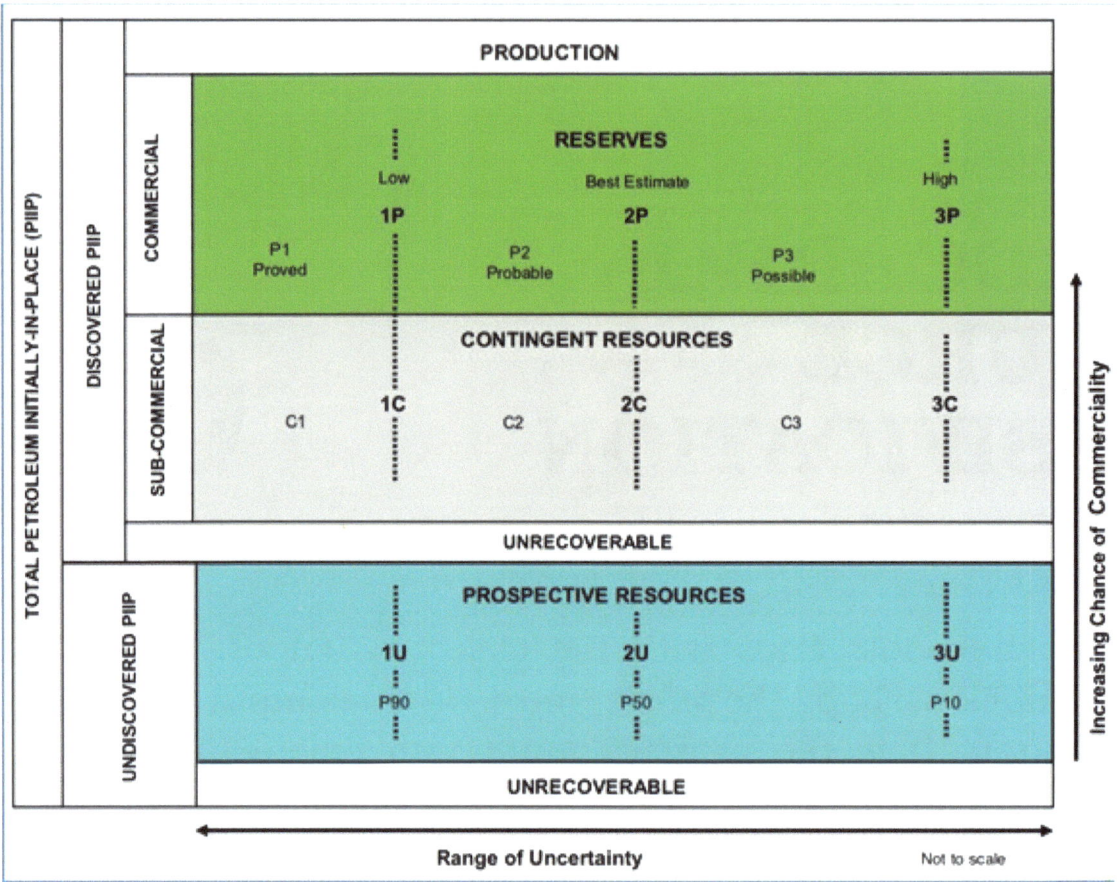

Figure 13: Hydrocarbon Resource Classification

The 'Range of Uncertainty' refers to a range of estimated quantities potentially recoverable from an accumulation by a project. This is a direct reflection of the state of maturation of the understanding of the accumulation. The vertical axis represents the "Chance of Commerciality", the probability that the project will be developed and reach commercially viable production status.

5.1 Total Petroleum Initially-In-Place (PIIP)

This is the quantity of petroleum that is estimated to exist originally in naturally occurring accumulations. It includes volumes contained in known accumulations prior to production as well as those yet to be discovered.

5.2 Discovered Petroleum Initially-In-Place

This represents the fraction of the PIIP contained in known accumulations prior to production.

Multiple development projects may be attached to each known accumulation, and each project will recover an estimated portion of the initially-in-place quantities. The projects are subdivided into Commercial and Sub-Commercial, with the estimated recoverable quantities being classified as Reserves and Contingent Resources respectively, as defined in Sections 5.5 and 5.6 respectively.

5.3 Undiscovered Petroleum Initially-In-Place

This is the fraction of the PIIP contained within accumulations yet to be discovered.

5.4 Production

Represents the cumulative quantity of petroleum that has been recovered on surface.

5.5 Reserves

Reserves are those quantities of petroleum anticipated to be commercially recoverable by execution of development projects under defined conditions. Reserves must further satisfy four criteria. They must be:

1. Discovered
2. Recoverable
3. Commercial
4. Remaining (i.e. not produced)

Reserve estimates are as of the evaluation date and based on the development project(s) attached. These volumes are further categorised in accordance with the level of certainty associated with the estimates. They may be sub-classified based on project maturity and/or characterised by development and production status as shown in Figure 14.

5.6 Contingent Resources

These are those quantities of petroleum estimated to be potentially recoverable from known accumulations, but the development project(s) are not yet considered mature enough for commercial recovery due to one or more contingencies.

Contingent Resources may include projects for which there are currently no viable markets, or where commercial recovery is dependent on technology under development, or where evaluation of the accumulation is insufficient to clearly assess commerciality.

This class of resources is further subdivided in accordance with the level of certainty associated with the estimates, project maturity and/or economic status.

5.7 Prospective Resources

These are those quantities of petroleum estimated to be potentially recoverable from undiscovered accumulations by application of future development projects. Prospective Resources, which have both an associated chance of discovery and development, are further sub-divided in accordance with the level of certainty associated with recoverable estimates assuming their discovery and development. They may also be sub-classified based on project maturity.

5.8 Unrecoverable resources

Unrecoverable resources are that portion of Discovered or Undiscovered Petroleum Initially-in-Place quantities which is estimated not to be recoverable by future development projects. A portion of these quantities may become recoverable in the future as commercial circumstances change or technological developments occur.

The remaining portion may never be recovered due to physical or chemical constraints represented by subsurface interaction of fluids and reservoir rocks.

5.9 Estimated Ultimate Recovery (EUR)

This is not a resource category, but a term that may be applied to any accumulation or group of discovered or undiscovered accumulations. It refers to those quantities of petroleum estimated to be potentially recoverable under defined technical and commercial conditions plus those quantities already produced.

5.10 Use of Hydrocarbon Resources Terminology

Table 2 presents a glossary of industry terms used in resource classification and commercial discussions.

Use of consistent terminology promotes clarity in communication and evaluation results. For Reserves, the general terms 'low', 'best' and 'high' are used to estimate the resulting 1P, 2P and 3P quantities, respectively. The associated incremental quantities are termed Proved (P1), Probable (P2) and Possible (P3).

Reserves must be viewed within the context of the complete resources classification system. While the categorisation criteria are mostly proposed for Reserves, the criteria can be equally applied to Contingent and Prospective Resources. Upon satisfying the commercial maturity criteria for discovery and/or development, the project quantities will then move to the appropriate resources sub-class.

Class	Definition
1C	Denotes the low estimate of Contingent Resources
2C	Denotes the best estimate of Contingent Resources
3C	Denotes a high estimate of Contingent Resources
1P	Denotes the minimum estimate of Reserves (Proved, P1 or P90 Reserves). It has the highest (Max) chance of occurrence.
2P	Denotes the best estimate of Reserves (Proved+Probable, P1+P2 or P50 Reserves). It has the most likely (ML) chance of occurrence.
3P	Denotes a high estimate of Reserves (Proved+Probable+Possible, P1+P2+P3 or P10 Reserves. It has the lowest (Min) chance of occurrence.
1U	Denotes the unrisked low estimate qualifying as Prospective Resources.
2U	Denotes the unrisked best estimate qualifying as Prospective Resources.
3U	Denotes the unrisked high estimate qualifying as Prospective Resources.

Table 2: Glossary of Terms Used in Hydrocarbon Resource Classification

5.11 Project Maturation Resource Sub-Classification

Development projects and associated recoverable quantities may be sub-classified (Figure 14) according to project maturity levels and the associated decision gate criteria required to move a project forward to commercial production. This approach supports the management of portfolios of opportunities at various stages of exploration, appraisal, and development.

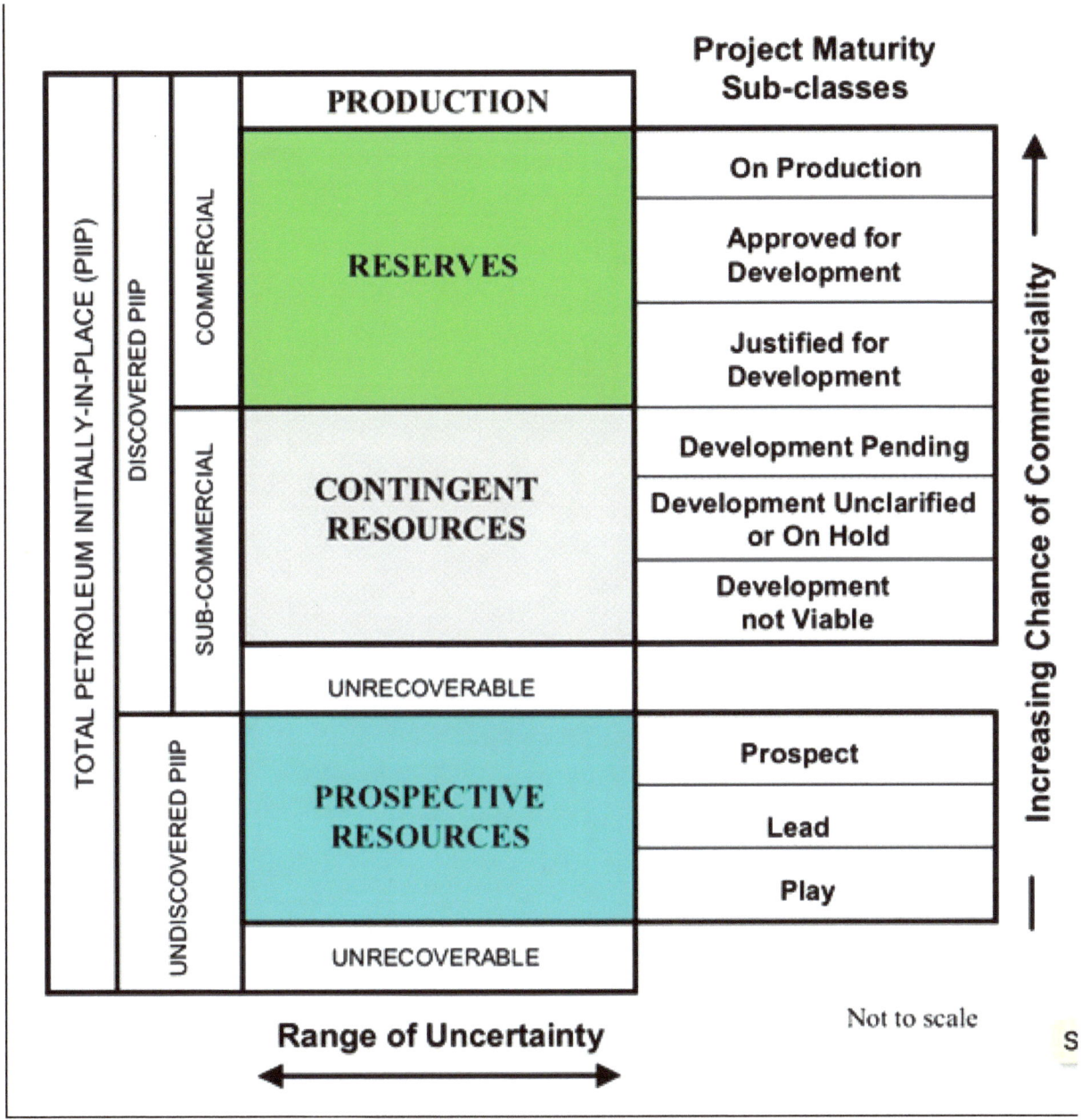

Figure 14: Resource Sub-Classes Based on Project Maturity

CHAPTER SIX
TERMINOLOGIES IN OIL AND GAS AGREEMENTS   06

This Section is a compilation of common terms and definitions of those terms used in the various agreements regulating the conduct and interactions of stakeholders in the Nigerian Oil and Gas industry. They are presented here in alphabetical order.

The upstream Manager is expected to be familiar with these terms because relationships between stakeholders (including HGs) often become litigious due to differences of opinion and the capital-intensive nature of the operations. The industry relies on these agreements and strict definitions in mediation.

Abandonment means all or any action or conduct for the purpose of ceasing operations and abandoning the wells and facilities installed in the Contract Area. This will usually happen under a respective agreement by way of demolition, removal, destruction, conversion, placement on temporary or permanent care and maintenance or any similar action or conduct and all other actions as are necessary to comply with relevant Government requirements of good oil field practice.

Accounting Procedure means the hydrocarbon and financial accounting rules, provisions and conditions set forth and contained in the named exhibit to a respective agreement.

AFE means an Authorisation for Expenditure pursuant to the respective Article in a particular agreement.

Affiliate means a company, partnership or other legal entity which controls, or is controlled by, or which is controlled by an entity which controls a Party, where 'Control' means the ownership directly or indirectly of more than fifty (50) percent of the voting rights in a company, partnership or legal entity.

Agreed Rate of Interest means interest compounded on a monthly basis, at the rate per annum according to terms agreed by the parties.

Agreement means a document, together with the exhibits attached and any extension, renewal or amendment agreed to in writing by the parties.

Appraisal Well means any well (other than an exploration or a development well) whose purpose at the time of commencement of drilling is to appraise the extent or the volume of petroleum reserves contained in an existing discovery.

Available Crude Oil means the crude oil won and saved from the contract area after deducting amounts used in petroleum operations.

Available Petroleum means the sum of available crude oil and available natural gas produced from the contract area less any oil or gas taken by way of royalty.

Available Natural Gas means the natural gas won and saved from the contract area after deducting amounts used in petroleum operations.

Barrel means a quantity consisting of forty-two (42) United States gallons, corrected to a temperature of sixty (60) degrees Fahrenheit under one (1) atmosphere of pressure.

Business Day means a day on which the banks in Nigeria and other specified countries are open for business.

Calendar Quarter means a period of three (3) months commencing with January 1 and ending on the following March 31; a period of three (3) months commencing with April 1 and ending on the following June 30; a period of three (3) months commencing with July 1 and ending on the following September 30; or a period of three (3) months commencing with October 1 and ending on the following December 31 according to the Gregorian Calendar.

Calendar Year means a period of twelve (12) months commencing from January 1 and ending on the succeeding December 31 according to the Gregorian Calendar.

Cash Premium means the payment made pursuant to the relevant Article by a Non-Consenting Party to reinstate its rights to participate in an Exclusive Operation (defined).

Capital Costs means all costs incurred pursuant to the Joint Operating Agreement and Concession prior to Payout. It shall include all costs which are not tax deductible in the year in which they are incurred together with any signature bonus, and any other analogous payment to the foregoing which are generally recognised as capital expenditure under the Regulations or by normal oil industry practice.

Collective Interest means a Party's Participating Interest, Paying Interest and Revenue Interest (defined).

Commercial Discovery means any discovery made in the contract area (defined) which the Operating Committee deems to have sufficient commercial worth to warrant the preparation and submission of a development plan in respect of such discovery to the Government for approval.

Completion means an operation intended to complete a well through the Christmas tree as a producer of Petroleum in one or more Zones, including, but not limited to, the setting of production casing, perforating, stimulating the well and production testing conducted in such operation. Complete and other derivatives are interpreted accordingly.

Consenting Party means a Party who agrees to participate in and pay its share of the cost of an Exclusive Operation.

Concession means the rights attached to the Contract Area, and any extensions, renewals or amendments agreed to in writing by the Parties and the Government together with those laws, statutes, rules and regulations with respect to exploration, development and production of petroleum that govern such instruments or are incorporated by the terms of such instruments.

Contract Area means the area as delineated by the coordinates in the relevant exhibit down to the depth referred to in the Agreement within the contract area and any greater depth to which the Parties may be entitled

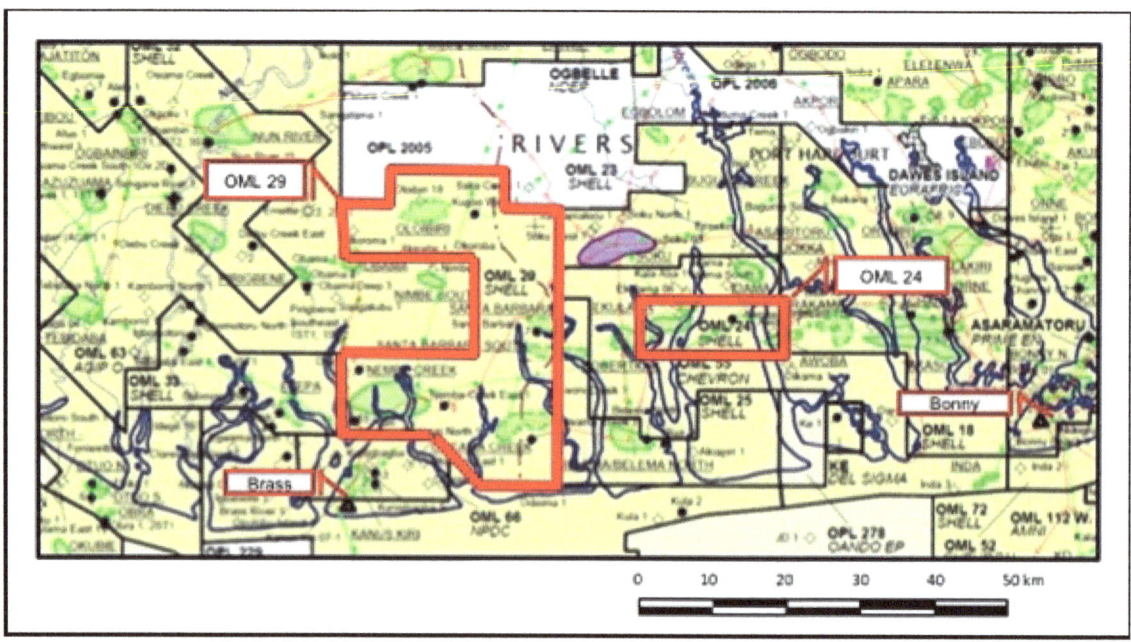

Figure 15: Typical Contract Area (courtesy IHS Energy)

to explore, develop and produce petroleum pursuant to the agreement referred to in the relevant Recital.

Crude Oil means liquid petroleum in its natural state before it has been refined or treated and includes condensate but excludes basic sediments and water.

Day means a calendar day unless otherwise specifically provided.

Default Interest Rate means:
(1) for amounts payable in US Dollars, interest compounded on a monthly basis, at the rate per annum equal to the one (1) month term, London Interbank Offered Rate (LIBOR) for US. Dollar deposits, as published by the Financial Times of London, plus X (usually 7-8) percentage points, applicable on the last business day prior to the due date of payment and thereafter on the last business day of each succeeding calendar month, and
(2) for amounts in default payable in local currency, the Nigerian Inter Bank Offered Rate (NIBOR) for overdrafts, advised by the Central Bank of Nigeria for the period in which the amount in default remains unpaid.

Deepening means an operation whereby a well is drilled to an objective zone below the deepest zone in which the well was previously drilled, or below the deepest zone proposed in the associated AFE, whichever is the deeper. Deepen and other derivatives are interpreted accordingly.

Development Plan means a plan for the development of petroleum from an exploitation Area.

Development Well means any well drilled for the production of petroleum pursuant to a development plan.

Discovery means the discovery of an accumulation of petroleum whose existence until that moment was unproven by drilling.

Dollars or $ means United States of America Dollars

Effective Date (of a Joint Operating Agreement - JOA) means the latter of the dates when
(I) the JOA, and all other documents in pursuance of the terms of the acquisition of an interest in the concession which require approval by the Government have been so approved; and
(ii) the JOA and all other documents as aforesaid requiring execution by the Parties have been executed.

Entitlement means a quantity of petroleum of which a Party has the right and obligation to take delivery pursuant to the concession under an offtake agreement, and the terms of this agreement, after adjustment for overlifts and underlifts.

Exclusive Operation means those operations and activities carried out pursuant to this agreement, the costs of which are chargeable to the account of less than all the Parties.

Exclusive Well means a well drilled pursuant to an Exclusive Operation.

Exploitation Area means that part of the contract area, which is established for development of a Commercial Discovery pursuant to the concession or if the concession does not establish an exploitation area, then that part of the Contract Area, which is delineated as the exploitation area in a Development Plan, approved as a Joint Operation or as an Exclusive Operation.

Exploitation Period means the period from the conversion of the OPL into an OML pursuant to the Regulations up to the date of the expiry of such OML.

Exploration Period means that period from the commencement of the concession up to the date the OPL is converted into an OML pursuant to the Regulations.

Exploration Well means any well whose purpose at the time of the commencement of drilling is to explore for an accumulation of petroleum whose existence was at that time unproven by drilling.

G&G Data means only geological, geophysical and geochemical data and other similar information that is not obtained through a well bore.

Government means the government of the Federal Republic of Nigeria and any political subdivision or agency or instrumentality thereof (including without limitation the Department of Petroleum Resources and the Ministry of Petroleum) with powers necessary to give effect to the terms and conditions of the JOA.

Gross Negligence means any act or failure to act (whether sole, joint or concurrent) by any person or entity which was intended to cause, or which was in reckless disregard of or wanton indifference to, harmful consequences where such person or entity knew, or should have known, such act or failure would have harmful consequences on the safety or property of another person or entity.

In Kind Premium means the grant of an interest in production made by a Non-Consenting Party to reinstate its rights under an Exclusive Operation.

Joint Account means the accounts in respect of the Joint Operations maintained in accordance with the provisions of the JOA and of the Accounting Procedure for Joint Operations.

Joint Operations means those operations and activities carried out by an Operator pursuant to the JOA, the costs of which are chargeable to all Parties according to their respective Paying Interests.

Joint Property means, at any point in time, all wells, facilities, equipment, materials, information, funds and the property held for use in Joint Operations.

Natural Gas means petroleum which is gaseous at atmospheric temperature and pressure including natural gas produced in association with crude oil or from reservoirs that produce mainly gaseous petroleum.

Net Proceeds means the proceeds less any royalty paid in cash.

Net Received Price means the actual price received by a Party upon sales of crude oil or natural gas net marketing costs (if any).

Non-Consenting Party means a Party who elects not to participate in an exclusive operation.

Operating Costs means those costs associated with or attributable to the production, treatment, transportation, storage or lifting of petroleum which are not recognised under the Regulations or by normal oil industry practice as capital costs.

Operator means Party and its successors and assigns designated as such in accordance with the agreement.

OML means an Oil Mining Lease issued by the Government.
OPL means an Oil Prospecting License issued by the Government.

Participating Interest means the undivided percentage interest of each Party in the ownership rights and obligations derived from the concession, the participation agreement and the JOA.

Party means any of the entities named in the commencement of an Agreement, its successors in title and any permitted assigns. Parties is interpreted accordingly.

Paying Interest means the respective obligations of the Parties to be liable for and to pay the costs and expenses associated with any and all

Joint Operations and expressed as a percentage of such costs and expenses, and calculated in accordance with the provisions of the relevant clause of the agreement.

Petroleum means crude oil and natural gas.

PPTA means the Petroleum Profits Tax Act, LFN 1990 and any amendment(s) thereto or any re-enactment(s) thereof.

Plugging Back means a single operation whereby a deeper zone is abandoned in order to attempt a completion in a shallower zone. Plug Back and other derivatives are interpreted accordingly.

Proceeds means the amount in Dollars determined by multiplying the net received price by the volume of available petroleum lifted by the relevant Party.

Recompletion means an operation whereby a completion in one zone is abandoned in order to attempt a completion in a different zone within the existing wellbore. Recomplete and other derivatives are interpreted accordingly.

Regulations means any laws, statutes and/or regulations which are applicable to the contract area and which govern the rights of any of the Parties.

Revenue Interest means the respective rights of the Parties to receive net proceeds produced from the contract area as a result of all Joint Operations conducted pursuant to the agreement and expressed as a percentage of such petroleum production and calculated in accordance with the provisions of the agreement.

Reworking means an operation conducted in a well after it is completed to secure, restore, or improve production in a zone which is currently open to production in the wellbore. Such operations include, but are not limited to, well stimulation operations, but exclude any routine repair or maintenance work, or drilling, sidetracking, deepening, completing, recompleting, or plugging back of a well. Rework and other derivatives are interpreted accordingly.

Royalty means the amount of royalty payable pursuant to the Petroleum Act, CAP. 350 Laws of the Federation of Nigeria and the Petroleum (Drilling and Production) Regulations made under CAP. 350, Laws of the Federation of Nigeria 1990, as amended from time to time.

Sidetracking means the directional control and intentional deviation of a well from vertical so as to change the bottom hole location unless done to straighten the hole or to drill around junk in the hole or to overcome other mechanical difficulties. Sidetrack and other derivatives are interpreted accordingly.

Stand-By Costs mean costs relating to operations conducted and incurred pursuant to the terms of a contract with a third-party contractor for the use of personnel, equipment or services during periods when such contractor is not actually providing the use of such personnel equipment or services but is still entitled to receive payment in respect thereof.

Tax means collectively, Petroleum Profits Tax, Niger Delta Development Commission (NDDC) levy and Education Tax and any other tax which may, from time to time, be imposed by the Government upon and in relation to the production of petroleum.

Technical Advisor means a Party and its successors and assigns designated as such in accordance with a Technical Services Agreement.

Technical Services Agreement means an agreement between parties under which one of the parties undertakes to provide assistance and training to others in the discharge of the functions required to conduct activities associated with exploration, appraisal, development and production of petroleum from the Concession.

Testing means an operation intended to evaluate the capacity of a zone to produce petroleum. Test and other derivatives are interpreted accordingly.

Work Obligations means those work and/or expenditure obligations specifed in the initial work program agreed by the Parties and attached as exhibit or in any subsequent work programme conducted under and pursuant to the Joint Operations.

Work Program and Budget means a work program and budget for Joint Operations as described and approved.

Zone means a stratum of earth containing or thought to contain an accumulation of petroleum separately producible from any other accumulation of petroleum.

Part Two

CHAPTER SEVEN

THE NIGERIAN UPSTREAM ENVIRONMENT   07

The upstream oil and gas organisational framework and the human resourcing of the resultant structure complement each other and form the engine room of the entire industry. This is where the rubber meets the road.

A day in the life of any upstream Manager would comprise interfaces with any number and combination of government organisations including, but not limited to the Department of Petroleum Resources (DPR), National Petroleum Investment Management Services (NAPIMS; a subsidiary of NNPC), the Nigerian National Petroleum Corporation (NNPC; corporate head office), the Nigerian Content Development and Monitoring Board (NCDMB) and the Nigerian Petroleum Exchange (NIPEX; a subsidiary of NAPIMS), just to name a few. Success or failure as an Operator in the Nigerian Oil and Gas space is determined largely by the establishment of the right interfaces with these organisations.

7.1 Government Agencies

In this Section, we shall attempt to define the framework for relationships between Operator and government agencies. We shall use the PSC regime as a template. The defined roles of the contractor group (represented by the Operator) and the concessionaire (NNPC/NAPIMS) within the PSCs and, to a large extent, the JVs are such that all project execution, quality assurance/control (QA/QC), capital expenditure (CAPEX) and operating expenditure (OPEX) is controlled by these agencies of government. The PSC provides for the establishment of a Management Committee (MACOM) made up of representatives from the different parties to the agreement. The purpose of the MACOM is to provide "orderly direction of all matters pertaining to petroleum operations and work program". The MACOM is traditionally chaired by the Group General Manager of NAPIMS or a designated representative and has oversight responsibility for all activities in the contract area. The powers and duties of the MACOM are outlined in the respective PSC documents.

A two-tier task force system is typically set up and subordinated to the MACOM. It is assigned the task of rudimentary oversight and provision of decision making inputs to MACOM. The first of these task forces is known as the Technical Committee (TECOM) composed along functional lines and populated with representatives from participating companies. The second prong of the two-tier task force structure are the sub-committees (SubCom). The number of SubComs established is dependent on the number of functional disciplines and determined at the behest of NAPIMS' management. In this hierarchical arrangement, the SubComs are a problem-solving organ and the output generated serves as input for the TECOM which, in turn, feeds the MACOM with recommendations from its deliberations for decision making.

The MACOM is expected to meet at least once every month and at such other times as may be mutually agreed, given proper notices. The meeting frequency for the TECOM and SubComs is determined based on the MACOM schedules. The decision gate timing and requirements are also tied to these formal meetings and could often be out of sync with what prevails in the operating companies. This divergence is a consequence of the preference for network organisations in the IOCs as opposed to the hierarchical and bureaucratic structures prevalent in the government agencies.

In this book, we recommend the adoption of network structures in government organisations and the reason is quite simple. The structure of the government agencies is traditionally hierarchical and therein lies one of the main constraints to establishing the much-desired networks required for efficient project deliveries. It is practically impossible to create seamless interfaces and plug-ins at the right levels between a networked and a hierarchical system.

7.2 Joint Teams and Interfaces

Some Independent Oil Companies (IOCs) and most of the smaller operating companies adopt a "What You See Is What You Get" (WYSIWYG) attitude to interface management between IOCs and agencies of government. This is a low risk approach to project delivery, especially given the peculiarities and relatively slow rate of evolution of the Nigerian Oil and Gas space.

One of our primary objectives in this book is to ensure that we do not leave our systems on autopilot. We must continue to seek ways to further engender a seamless interface between joint teams which are made up of individuals from markedly different organisational cultures. This we describe as a "Hybrid Network Model" or, simply put, the HN Model.

7.2.1 Characteristics of the HN Model

The first thing to note is that the HN Model is an interface model. But it differs from the traditional interface management protocols in the sense that it actually recognises and takes account of the aforementioned peculiarities of organisational behaviour. It allows collaborating parties maintain their respective cultures whilst developing enhancements to existing routines with an ultimate goal for convergence over time. The industry needs to develop Managers who:

1. Recognise and capture the full range of possible outcomes at every decision gate
2. Are conscious of the need to maintain a tightly coupled organisation despite the inherent vagaries. The organisation must have a set of mutually understood rules backed by a quality assurance system. The Manager must conform to specific workflow guidelines.

7.2.2 The Manager's Working Environment

In a traditional non-networked organisation, Managers pull data, details and facts from outside the organisation and from the Supervisors below. After processing, relevant information is pushed up to the layer above them. They directly manage the workers and take responsibility for the day-to-day operations of the business. They take daily information from the Supervisors below them, and report summaries of the data to the higher level of Management. Often described as "Middle Managers", they are the influencers and decision makers sitting between top management above and supervisors below.

It is important to note that Managers also deal with goal setting and department level decision making. They, therefore need to get summarised information across functional lines, within and outside their respective organisations, periodically. A hybrid environment by its very nature is often not amenable to synchronised activity or fast and efficient turnaround.

The role of a Manager in such an environment is, therefore, to ensure accurate bi-directional information flow as well as vertical and horizontal deliveries to meet corporate goals and objectives. It is this positional functionality that has given rise to the expression 'The Role in the Middle'.

To set the scene for a discourse on the limitations of a hybrid work environment and possible optimisation options, we need a clear understanding of a traditional (non-networked) upstream structure. An example is shown in Figure 16. The four typical functional lines are:

1 Exploration and Production Operations
2 Drilling Operations and Drilling Engineering
3 Petroleum and Production Engineering
4 Finance and Commercial

Each functional 'line' is headed by a Manager who is responsible for a respective area, as well as for specialised units within these functional lines. The Manager is well positioned to receive strategic information from above and data from below to track progress and current conditions.

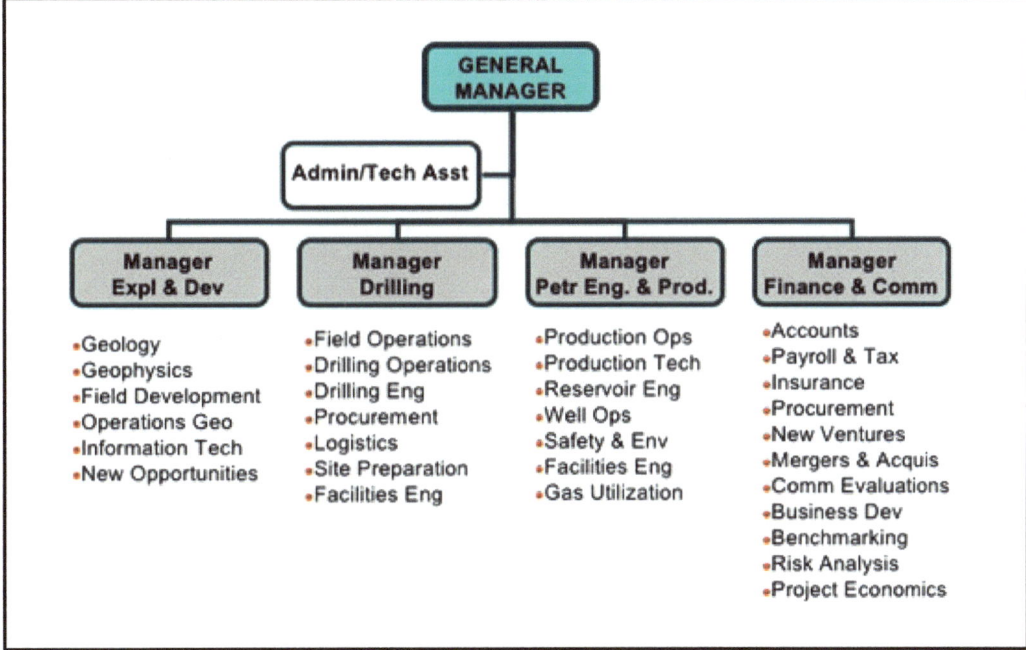

Figure - 16: Traditional Exploration and Production Organisation

In this type of environment, the Managers spend 80% of their time interpreting and implementing strategies for reaching organisational objectives set by top management. The risk of exposure to a misaligned hybrid environment for decision making is very high, hence the advocacy for tightly coupled organisations as the minimum. A fully networked environment should however remain the desired and ultimate goal.

The term 'Strategy' is a military term that has been adopted in business circles and by the general populace. It is helpful to think of strategy as the plan to change the environment from its current state to a new, desired state. In a healthy organisation, strategy does not change in the short term.

'Processes', on the other hand, can be seen as steps towards achievement of strategic goals and incorporates cross-functional plans and results. Processes specifically refer to how to achieve the desired outcomes and may change as conditions require.

Constant and accurate flow of information must be maintained by the Manager. The interplay of technology, IT systems and organisational structure must be clearly defined and functionality guaranteed. A high performing organisation must ensure zero tolerance on losses attributed to downtime on information flow.

A typical information flow network is shown in Figure 17.

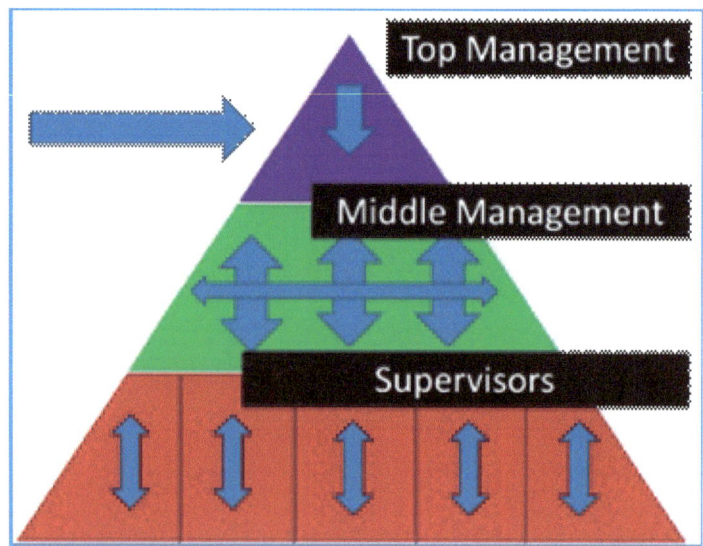

Figure - 17: Management Information Flow (courtesy study.com)

In Section 7.3, we will examine how Managers have to function in the light of different roles. The purpose is to clarify how you as a Manager should relate to your surroundings, your team and network in particular, as well as how you adopt different roles depending on the situation and the expectations of your surroundings. This is not unlike an actor who must convince an audience (our surroundings at work), and themselves that they are authentic.

As a Manager, you adopt a role that is imposed on you. You thus have the opportunity to determine what you want others to see. Your behaviour as Manager should correspond as far as possible with the expectations of your audience. Your credibility as a Manager is often dependent on your ability to ensure that your behaviour remains congruent with expectations. You must walk the talk.

7.3 Roles and Personality

Roles are distinct from personalities to the extent that roles in a team are mostly fixed while the person can be replaced. The stage metaphor is therefore an appropriate one. The 'actor' is the Manager, while the role is the 'script'. The role of a Manager exists in the same way as a script is available for the actor.

As a Manager, you have to give life to the role, fill it with your personality and give it credibility and content.

To understand the role of a Manager, we will start with the organisation's expectations. Explicit and implicit expectations of your role as a Manager must be mapped. By first examining the role as an 'empty vessel' you will be able to grasp the various formal and informal expectations of your position.

7.4 Roles and Networks

Networks often designate the distribution of people across the boundaries defined by the usual structures. This refers primarily to two main areas:

1. Relationships and collaborations across the boundaries of functional (professional) and structural (line organisation) silos.
2. Relationships and collaborations in joint teams with government agencies especially as required by MACOM, TECOM and the SubCom.

Roles in networks are therefore commonly regarded as being unusual. We will examine more closely what network roles entail for individuals.

Networks form an important part of our daily work and these structures are important for production, efficiency, learning and social life. The roles in a network thus correspond in many ways to the more traditional and formal roles to be found in respective companies. At the same time, network roles differ from more traditional ones primarily because behaviour in networks entails continuous shifts in terms of authority and communication patterns.

You will get a more comprehensive understanding of your role as Manager and increase your ability to lead through:

1. Understanding your own role in relation to your surroundings
2. The formal job requirements
3. The organisation's expectations
4. Networks

To a large extent, success is dependent on your ability to make the most of the potentials in networks. This will help you achieve both your personal and organisation's goals. Remember: your role is what you make of it.

7.5 Organisational Structure

Unlike traditional organisations which are divided into four main functional segments, a fully networked system is hinged upon the philosophy that a healthy organisation is not an "either or" but an all-inclusive entity.

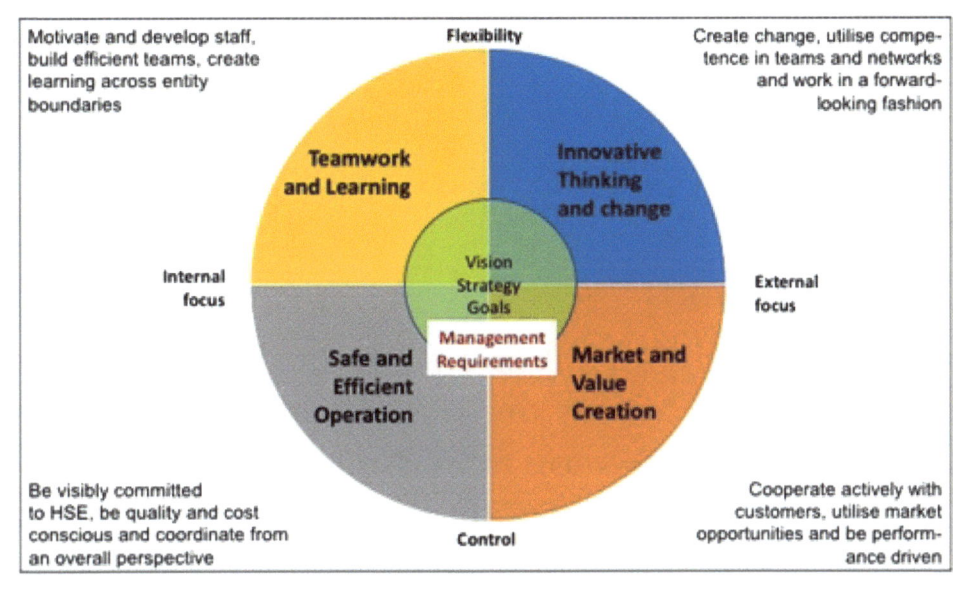

Figure - 18: Organisational Segments

These four main functional segments are described below:

1. **Market and Value Creation:** setting goals, generating results, following up action plans, and customer service
2. **Safe and Efficient Operation:** strong focus on HSE, measuring and efficiently following up operations, and coordinating across organisational boundaries.
3. **Teamwork and Learning:** provide feedback to staff, communicate clearly and openly, listen actively, master 'difficult conversations', build confidence and trust, optimise staff competence, learn from mistakes, pass on and bring in selected members of staff, ensure good interaction and a good atmosphere.

4. **Innovative Thinking and Change:** discover and try out new possibilities, support renewal and change, develop and use networks, liaise with Managers from other parts of the organisation, share relevant practice, develop visions and plans, look ahead, communicate goals and visions, be aware of company's role in society.

A fully networked organisation would exhibit four out of four (4/4 = 100%) of these functional attribute groupings within broad boundaries. Does your organisation fit this profile? If so, your role as a Manager is made simple in the sense that all you need to do is to keep maintaining the balance.

If, on the other hand, your organisation's score is skewed towards 50% or less (i.e. prominent in two or only one out of four groupings), you as a Manager must, with support from top management, identify the areas of weakness and design soft goals for your team members to bridge the gaps. This is the first step in developing an efficient and fully networked organisation.

7.6 Leadership Styles

The four organisational segments described in Section 7.5 are closely related to the behaviour and competencies expected of Managers. On the basis of the efficiency criteria (key results areas) listed above, we can envisage four Leadership Styles (Competency Areas) for Managers.

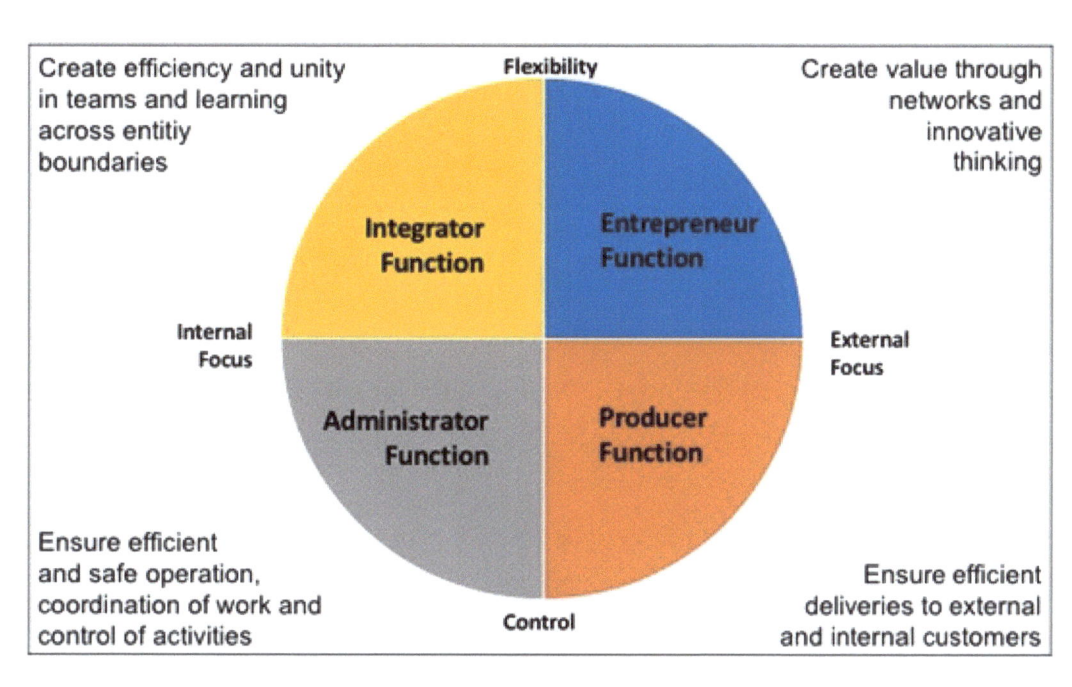

Figure 19: Competency Model for Managers

Similar to what is described for the functional groupings in Section 7.5, most competency models for Managers are based on a framework which states that effective and efficient leadership is about having balanced competence in the different areas. These areas are placed as quadrants in the model in Figure 19 and are based on four important aspects of organisational theory, management and culture.

Traditionally, the quadrants have been regarded as separate units. In the network model, they will be viewed as competing goals which Managers and organisations must work towards. Thus, it is not an "either or" model, but rather one in which the Manager must find a balance among the four segments.

A Manager in a fully efficient networked organisation would exhibit four out of four (4/4 = 100%) of the competencies within broad margins. If, on the other hand, your competencies are skewed towards 50% or less (i.e. prominent in two or only one out of four), you as a Manager must identify the areas of weakness and work to bridge the gaps. This should form part of your personal development plan going forward.

7.7 Management Paradoxes

Managers will experience paradoxes and contradictions among the different quadrants. One example may be between the administrative function and the entrepreneurial or innovative function. On one side, there is a need for continuity and control while the opposite axis will strive towards creativity and flexibility. A corresponding axis of contradictions is to be found between the market and producer functions and the integrator and people-orientation.

In the following sub-sections, we will look deeper into the Manager's behaviour and leadership role in relation to the different corporate functional segments.

7.8 Role Definition Exercise

Your choice on how you should behave as a Manager will not always be in tandem with other people's perceptions and expectations. That notwithstanding, it is important that you adopt a conscious attitude to the different expectations and broad spectrum of role requirements that exist.

In this section, you will carry out a personal evaluation based on the following four steps:

a) Self-assess your dominant competence based on current top 10 tasks. You will be required to describe the expectations others may have of you in your role as a Manager.
b) Based on the competence model (section 7.6), map what you perceive to be the performance expectations of the functional roles described in section 7.5.
c) Compare results from A (self-assessment of current role) and B (expectation). Note any gaps between the two.
d) Prepare a Personal Development Plan to bridge the gaps, where applicable.

This is a more detailed and insightful exercise than the broad one carried out in Section 7.6. The outcomes of both exercises should however be in alignment.

Detailed instructions and guidelines are provided in ensuing sections 7.8.1 to 7.8.10.

In this exercise, you will self-analyse of your role as Manager in relation to the competence model for managers described in Section 7.6 above.	List in order of importance up to 10 of your key duties. Give an indication of the percentage of the working hours spent on each task. Total = 100%:
Task: Remember, your own and others' perceptions and expectations of how you should behave as a Manager are not always in the same . They do not necessarily have to be in sync but it is important that you adopt a conscious attitude to the different expectations and role requirements that exist. In this exercise, you are required to describe what you think others expect of you in your role as a Manager.	1) 2) 3) 4) 5) 6) 7) 8) 9) 10)

Table 3 Task Overview of Current Role Self-Analysis

To be used in conjunction with guidelines on Table 3 (self-analysis) and in relation to your 'top 10' list. **Focus on the more relevant questions to your role and present your summarised answers and % assessment in Figure 20.**

INTEGRATOR	ENTREPRENEUR
• How would you evaluate your performance in creating the right working environment within your organisation and ensure a rating >4.5 (1 being 'Poor' and 5 being 'Excellent')? • How would you define collaboration? Based on your attitude, do you think the word collaboration means what it should to you? • What would you do differently to increase collaboration?	• How well should you promote the ideas from your team up to you? • What areas of improvement would you suggest to guarantee better flow of information and effective communication between you and your team members? • "I am willing to try new solutions and methods but a bit unsure what my limits are." How would you define the boundaries?
ADMINISTRATOR	**PRODUCER**

• What is expected of you as a leader in the future?
• What, in your opinion, are the most important criteria for success in your current position?
• What keyword would you select to describe your function; why/why not?
   ➢ Innovative (entrepreneur)
   ➢ Efficient (producer)
   ➢ Coordinator (administrator)
   ➢ Team player (integrator)
	• How do you react or deal with the consequences when your pace of delivery affects you negatively?
	• How would you evaluate your performance in articulating the business plan with respect to your organisation's performance targets?

Table 4 Current Role Self-Analysis Questionnaire

7.8.1 Characteristics of The Entrepreneur Function

Evaluate your role as Manager using the role characteristics described in this sub-section 7.8.1 in relation to the questions and guidelines in sub-section 7.8.2 and **present your summary in the box provided.**

Keywords:

- Creative
- Communicator
- Risk taker
- Follows up
- Provides feedback
- Experiments
- Problem solver
- Change manager
- Brings in resources
- Networks
- Adopts long term perspective
- Speaker
- Motivator
- Creator of opportunities
- Focus on company values and role in society

Characteristics:

Managers who excel in the entrepreneurial function often come up with new ideas, experiment with new concepts, are creative in solving problems and are continuously on the lookout for improvements and innovations.

Managers in this quadrant are often visionary and cultivate the distinctive and unique. They are in close contact with external networks and bring these connections into the organisation.

They are often characterised by their challenge of the status quo and contributing a fresh perspective. Managers who excel in the entrepreneurial function initiate and implement change.

7.8.2 Expectations for the Entrepreneur Function

In performing my role as an Entrepreneur Manager, to what extent am I expected to:

1. **react positively to change:** encourage and support innovative thinking; actively instigate renewal and restructuring; redefine problems as opportunities.

2. **instigate changes when required:** initiate creative processes and new projects; create ownership of these initiatives in the organisation (both upwards and downwards), and follow up.
3. **show willingness to try new solutions and methods:** occasionally take big chances in order to promote restructuring; come up with new ideas; have the competence required for promoting creative processes in the team.
4. **challenge the status quo:** see and exploit new opportunities; introduce new perspectives; adopt a way of thinking that challenges the status quo and express the new.
5. **have a clear external focus:** carry out negotiations; initiate meetings and represent the company externally; act as a link to customers and suppliers while maintaining important connections within the organisation.
6. **build networks in order to 'achieve things':** stay in regular contact with managers in other parts of the enterprise; master the 'informal channels'; exercise a large degree of influence; use different people to acquire knowledge and information; provide others with and bring in resources as required.

On the basis of the questions, specify what you perceive to be the expectations of how you should perform the entrepreneur function. **Present your summary of the GAPS with respect to your current performance in Figure 21.**

7.8.3 Characteristics of The Producer Function

Evaluate your role as Manager using the role characteristics described in this sub-section 7.8.3 in relation to the questions and guidelines in sub-section 7.8.4 and **present your summary in the box provided.**

Keywords:

- Task oriented
- Market and customer focus
- Efficient
- Opportunity oriented
- Responsible for results
- Performance focussed
- Competitive
- Proactive
- Positive/energetic attitude
- Highly motivated
- Encouraging
- Decisive
- Goal oriented
- Strategic planning
- Delegation
- Organisation
- Prioritises clearly

Characteristics:

The organisation must demonstrate its value by delivering something to its surroundings. Managers in this function are expected to direct their activities towards goals and be accountable for results. They are logical problem solvers who are good at handling deadlines and stress.

Efficient managers in this function achieve results through creating performance-oriented working environments and concern themselves with competition and external threats. They have a lot of positive energy, and customer contracts are often celebrated as achievements and victories.

They communicate clear expectations. They plan well and set clear goals for others. Their own concern with producing results means that they are often role models. They have a clear idea of what must be done and what can be left until later.

7.8.4 Expectations for the Producer Function

In performing my role as a Producer Manager, to what extent am I expected to:

1. **be goal-oriented and concerned with making progress:** make sure that meetings are decision-oriented and effective; have clear ambitions and goals.
2. **understand the market, forces for change, competitors and own position:** argue internally from a customer standpoint. Use competition to create drive
3. **win customers' trust and respect:** take customer complaints seriously, understand customer needs and preferences; follow up customers.
4. **respond consistently to performances and behaviour:** take on the role of 'fair judge' at times.
5. **break down strategy into clear goals that are followed up:** effectively communicate goals and strategies; follow up individual staff members; make performance measurement standard clear.
6. **allocate tasks and efficiently organise available resources:** define roles and expectations; be clear about priorities; distribute tasks evenly; organise responsibility and authority so that effort and competence building are stimulated.

On the basis of the questions, specify what you perceive to be the expectations of how you should perform the producer function. **Present your summary of the GAPS with respect to your current performance in Figure 21.**

7.8.5 Characteristics of The Administrator Function

Evaluate your role as Manager using the role characteristics described in this sub-section 7.8.5 in relation to the questions and guidelines in sub-section 7.8.6 and **present your summary in the box provided.**

Keywords:
- Uncompromising attitude to HSE
- Rule-oriented
- Follow up rule violations
- Efficient control
- Utilise resources
- Planning
- Ambitious performance
- Anticipate problems
- Control and measurement
- Reliability
- Organisation
- Job design
- Evaluating
- Concerned with detail
- Analysis
- Coordination
- System perspective

Characteristics:

Organisation (verb) means the systematic solution of repetitive tasks. The administrator function entails establishing and operating systems that ensure a high degree of regularity and efficiency in production. Management tasks will often involve detailed planning, coordination, laying down rules and procedures, evaluating operation and results and checking that the team and staff are utilising resources efficiently.

An efficient manager in this function has a good overview and anticipates problems in the workflow. He or she is concerned with achieving smooth interaction across staff and departmental boundaries.

Discovering mistakes, pointing out obligations, maintaining a good overview and structure are all important aspects of the administrator function. The manager checks, evaluates, monitors and picks up signs of non-compliance in the organisation.

7.8.6 Expectations for the Administrator Function

In performing my role as an Administrator Manager, to what extent am I expected to:

1. **maintain a good overview of the organisation's activities:** seldom taken by surprise by 'new information'. Know where to go to obtain resources, knowledge and information.
2. **have projects under control:** immediately deal with the situation if anything goes wrong. Recruit and allocate the 'right' resources to the 'right' tasks; actively check that everyone performs their assigned tasks; master management tools.
3. **ensure compliance with budgets and spending limits:** set a good example for own staff in terms of being cost-conscious; emphasise cost focus in own entity; emphasise cost benefit thinking in prioritising and planning.
4. **create synergies across boundaries:** avoid sub-optimisation; achieve learning across boundaries; talk about best practice and quality systems; initiate actions across boundaries; share knowledge with others.
5. **obtain crucial information for making decisions:** absorb complicated information; distinguish the important from the unimportant; verify data.
6. **check progress and pass this information on:** communicate milestones, non-conformity, change and progress status to the entity, department and team.

On the basis of the questions, specify what you perceive to be **the** expectations of how you should perform the administrator function. **Present your summary of the GAPS with respect to your current performance in Figure 21.**

7.8.7 Characteristics of The Integrator Function

Evaluate your role as Manager using the role characteristics described in this sub-section 7.8.7 in relation to the questions and guidelines in sub-section 7.8.8 and **present your summary in the box provided.**

Keywords:

- Active listener
- Challenges and integrates
- Inclusive and available
- Clarifies
- Conflict resolution
- Community and team building
- Focus on process and group dynamics
- Empathy and understanding
- Human resources
- Team building
- Fairness
- Interpersonal communication

Characteristics:

Nowadays, organisations need to be held together by employees who choose voluntarily to be part of them and want to make a personal contribution. The need to create a social and working community that provides meaning and context for the individual is important. This is referred to as the integrator function.

Efficient managers in this function focus on creating effective interaction between people in teams and departments. They intervene and deal with conflicts, master the art of dialogue, are concerned with community, but also focus on individuals' needs and development (growth environment).

Important aspects of this function include focusing on the individual and demonstrating that people constitute the organisation's most important resource for achieving its goals.

7.8.8 Expectations for the Integrator Function

In performing my role as an Integrator Manager, to what extent am I expected to:

a) **contribute to the development of a good team spirit and good cooperation in the department/team:** be capable of intervening when the team gets stuck; utilise the diversity within the group; concerned with the entity's social life.

b) **create commitment and enjoyment of work:** communicate in such a fashion that you build a community, take a clear stand on specific matters. Be clear and to the point; celebrate 'victories'. Share positive experiences. Assign tasks that require the staff to extend themselves.

c) **create good conditions for learning and development among staff:** maintain a good overview of different preferences and resources; assign challenging tasks.

d) **master the art of dialogue: listen to staff without interrupting;** provide clear and understandable feedback. Contribute to and be constructive in discussions.

e) **bring conflicting parties together:** show courage in conflict situations; do not postpone conflicts and difficult conversations; be a mediator.

f) **be a model for others: maintain high ethical standards;** be inclusive. Put in effort; show consideration and care.

On the basis of the questions, specify what you perceive to be **the** expectations of how you should perform the integrator function. **Present your summary of the GAPS with respect to your current performance in Figure 21.**

7.8.9 Summary of Current Role Self-Analysis

** Competence Balance Assessment – CBA (%) =

Figure 20: Current Role Self Analysis

7.8.10 Summary of Revised Role Analysis

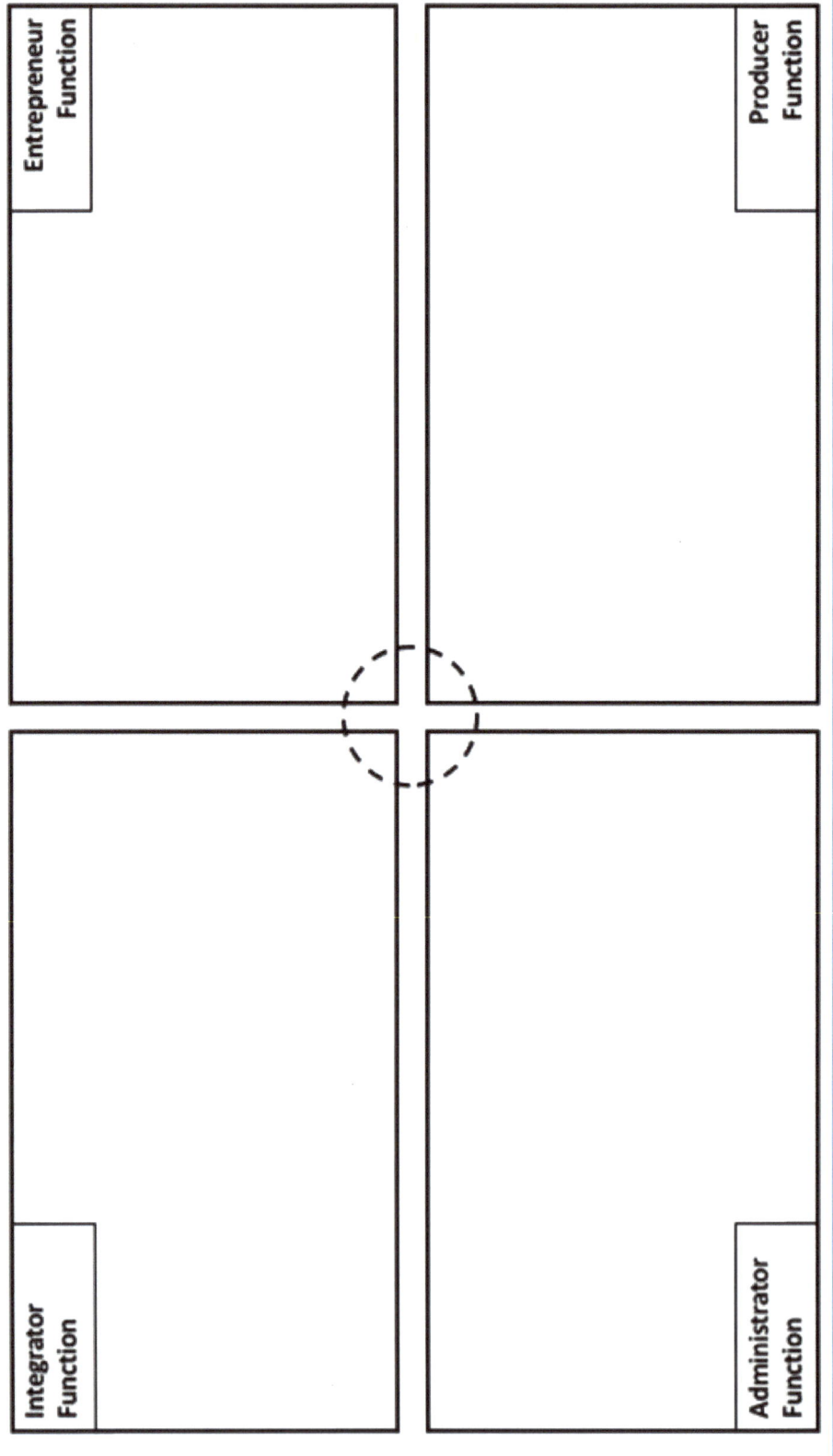

Figure 21: Revised Role Analysis

7.9 Management in Teams and Networks

In this part of the book we shall look more closely at networks and special network roles.

Networks are often perceived as being informal organisations within, outside or cutting across the boundaries of organisations and entities. Focus on networks has increased recently and there is a clear tendency for networks to be formalised and in many cases given a place on organisational charts. The reason for this is the recognition of the power and resources that lie in well-functioning networks.

Networks exist in various forms and for various purposes. Common to them all is that they always have a purpose or a clear goal. In the network pyramid model, the different dimensions of networks are stipulated. The starting point is the individual who has a goal or purpose for their participation in networks.

The sum of these individual goals is the network's goal. In working towards the goal, individuals use different tools and knowledge. A network also comprises the other participants who are part of this community. The community is governed by norms and rules. A network must also have a certain division of labour to achieve its goal.

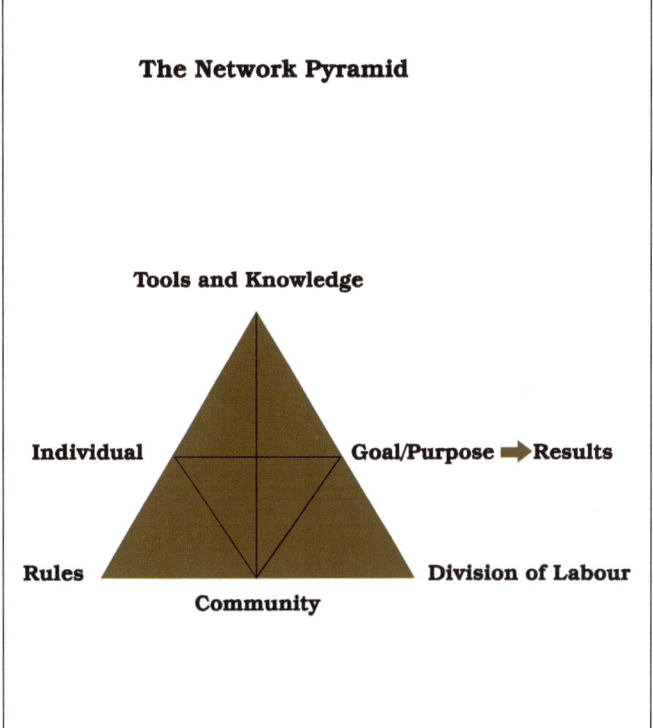

7.9.1 Network Roles

The different persons taking part in a network will have different functions and roles. The distribution of roles will often be a result of the network's purpose and goal. An uneven distribution of roles will, as a rule, be dysfunctional for the network.

In networks, roles often change and participants operate under different communication and authority patterns than they are used to. In the top model on the right, the network pyramid is divided into the network's functions and activities. **Innovative thinking and change** constitute the element of innovation engaged in by the network. The second element, **network building**, is the social dimension which is governed by norms and rules. **Goal orientation** is the network's regulation of the purpose and direction of activities. **Production** describes the network and what it is in fact engaged in. There is a role pertaining to each network function. Participants in the network play these roles through their involvement and actions vis-a-vis the network.

Taking part in networks is about operating at the juncture between everyday operations in the entity and participation in network activities. It is an important point that networks should enrich and strengthen you in your role as a manager in relation to your entity, just as you bring along your competence and skills to strengthen the rest of the organisation through your participation in networks.

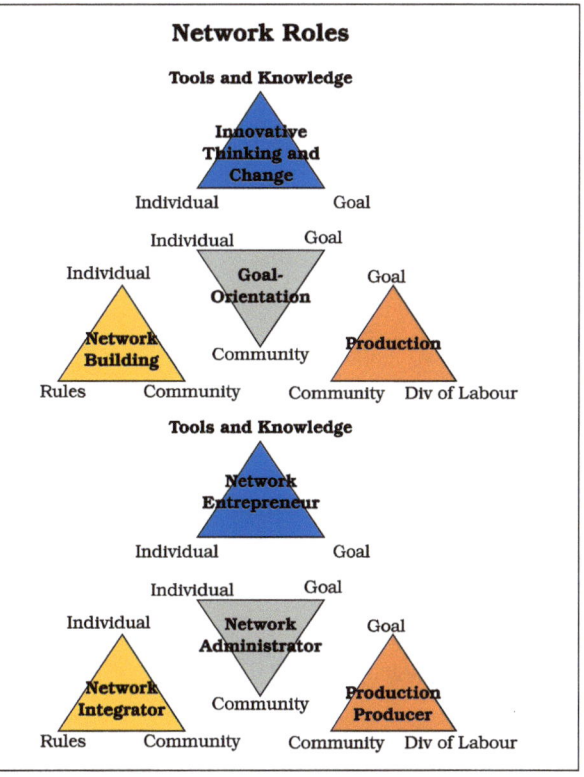

7.9.1.1 The Network Entrepreneur

Tools and Knowledge

[Triangle diagram: Network Entrepreneur, with vertices Individual and Goal]

Keywords:
- Innovative thinking
- Shares new knowledge
- Systematises experiences and develops them innovatively
- Discovers new efficient methods
- Follows up initiatives
- Creates opportunities
- Thinks in broad and creative terms
- Acquires new knowledge for own entity
- Thinks ahead

Description
In networks, innovative thinking and change are about bringing out, obtaining, exchanging and developing tools, working methods and knowledge in the network. Innovation and innovative thinking are central to the achievement of organisation's goals, both in one's own and others' teams and entities.

Usual Challenges
Networks are characterised by knowledge being situated internally in the different layers, making them dependent on the participation of key persons. The working methods employed daily by the different members are developed through internal trial and error. One should endeavour to acquire the tools and knowledge possessed by other entities and which can improve activity in one's own entity. The knowledge and tools in the team's possession are adapted to its work tasks and routines rather than to its goals. Individual focus will mostly be on everyday operations (and not on developing knowledge and skills) that are forward-looking and oriented towards better goal achievement.

7.9.1.2 The Network Integrator

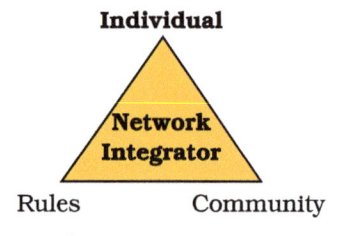

Keywords:
- Creates procedures for learning in networks
- Shares knowledge
- Seeks cooperation between entities
- Systematises experiences
- Gets resources to work together
- Realises the value of the social aspects of the network
- Creates arenas for learning across entity boundaries
- Realises the value of the network's activity
- Has an overview of innovation in the organisation

Description
Network-building is a key element in achieving well-functioning learning and development across entity boundaries. Network integrators establish rules and systems for exchanging knowledge and experiences, thereby creating a framework for learning and development. The networks' role is very much about building a culture which underpins corporate goals. The network integrator sees the whole of the organisation as a joint body working towards the same goals.

Usual challenges
Network building will often be characterised by top down implementation of rules for collaboration. Involvement in and commitment to participation for the common good may be difficult to achieve. There will often be 'solo participants' who are more concerned with their own efforts and rewards than with the common good. It may be difficult to establish good procedures for teamwork in a network since these often come on top of everyday duties. It will often be difficult to obtain an overview of innovation and what the different entities are engaged in.

7.9.1.3 The Network Administrator

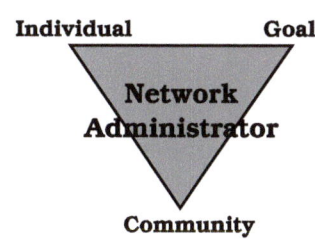

Keywords:
- Establishes a vision of what the network aims to achieve
- Evaluates the usefulness of activities
- Views the network's role in a wider context
- Helps individuals make contributions to the network
- Ensures that the network is meaningful and valuable to its participants
- Coordinates activities

Description
Network administration is about creating networks that are expedient for individuals, entities and the organisation. It is a central task to establish goals for activities in the network and coordinate activities around these goals. This role also entails evaluating networks as well as their usefulness in relation to effort and costs invested and viewing networks in a wider context.

Usual challenges
It may be difficult to get networks to understand the purpose of coordinated action and to get participants to adopt a shared focus and direction. It is important to strike a balance between effort, desire and personal commitment and focusing on goals, direction and the functional framework. In networks, there will often be no clear, formal roles. Disagreements can easily arise between different administrator roles. There are often few sanctions available in the event of conflicts.

7.9.1.4 The Network Producer

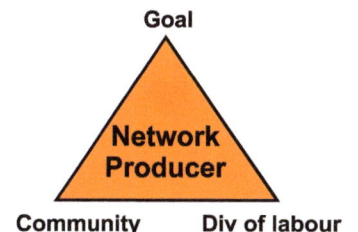

Keywords:
- Follows up goals through concrete activities
- Utilises resources in the network
- Distributes tasks on the basis of the members' diverse knowledge and experience
- Ensures that network production is transferred to own entity
- Draws on own entity's competence in production
- Ensures that the network's production creates value for the organisation

Description
A network's production is a result of the skills possessed by the network's community and how these are distributed through the division of labour to achieve the team's goal. The division of labour should be expedient in terms of achieving the goal. It is important, therefore, to have an overview of the resources at the disposal of the community and the network.

Usual challenges
It is often difficult to achieve a balanced division of labour in a community that will cover all the tasks that must be performed to achieve the goals. If production does not meet the goals, it will be problematic to change the composition of the community or the division of labour. Since a network often has an enjoyable, voluntary dimension, it is difficult to stipulate stringent requirements for concrete work in networks.

CHAPTER EIGHT

SOFT SKILLS FOR THE MANAGER

08

In this section, we shall consider issues related to the following questions:

1. If I am lonely as a leader, should I conclude there is something wrong?
2. Why is it so critical that I lead myself well?
3. What is the quickest way to evaluate how well I am leading my team?

4. How do I lead the toughest person on my team?
5. How do I avoid losing key people?

We shall only scratch the surface of each issue in this book. Our goal is to identify tangible takeaways to raise the readers leadership standard in the short term. The subject matter shall include the following:

- Inclusive leadership
- How to lead yourself
- How to handle criticism
- The leader's first responsibility
- Leaders never stop learning
- How to be a leader worth following
- Leadership legacy

It has been said that a **wise** person learns from his mistakes. A **wiser** person learns from other's mistakes. But the **wisest** person of all learns from other's successes. Experience has shown that leadership makes a big difference, either good or bad. Everything rises and falls with leadership.

Charlie Brown, the main character in the very popular and long-tenured comic strip Peanuts typifies a loser and yet a leader who rises out of every downfall with shining hope and determination. In one of the strips, he stood on the beach admiring a sand castle he had built only to have it levelled by heavy rainfall. As he looked at the smooth place where his artwork had once stood, he said, "There must be a lesson here, but I don't know what it is."

How many times has your "sand castle" been wiped out, with all or part of your team in it, yet you never learnt a thing? For those who may be privy to my antecedents, I have acquired experience as an Oil and Gas specialist spans some four (4) decades and different continents. Do you think that makes me an expert?

Perhaps it does. But it hardly feels that way simply because good leaders never stop learning. I made my first leadership error 14 years into my career soon after I returned from my first international assignment. The eventual outcome belongs in history but the point that needs to be made here is that I did not even realise until recently that it was a leadership error and not the direct consequence of a job change which occurred about the same time. The details are beyond the scope of this book but available to interested persons who sign up for our coaching or mentorship programs.

8.1　Inclusive Leadership

A good leader does not leave everyone behind and take the journey to the top alone. Taking people to the top is what good leaders do.

Question: What do we need to know about taking people to the top?

The truth is that no one ever gets to the top alone. If you are a leader in your organisation, you probably did not get there all by yourself. The tragic mistake some make is that they get protective of the position they attained through teamwork and choose to supress others.

It is similar to playing the 'King of the Hill' game. It is a popular game with children, and the reason is not far-fetched. The rules of the game, which comes in many variants, is such that a single individual who makes it to the top of the 'hill' will deploy every weapon in his/her arsenal to deny anyone else access to the 'throne'. Children therefore love to play this game. Adults too are enamoured by the rules of this game and quite often deploy it in the workplace.

If you are lonely at the top, you should evaluate your behaviour. You may be clinging to your position rather than connecting with your colleagues for more efficient deployment of the team's resources. You must create a growth environment to enable them to join you at the top. We shall expatiate on the concept of a growth environment in Section 8.5 and in even greater detail in our mentorship programs for those who sign up for them. For the context of this book, simply remember that a live and active succession plan actually facilitates your own growth and development as a leader.

If you are lonely as a leader, interrogate yourself by asking the question; "what is wrong?" This is a great question to ask. Some leaders think that they are lonely at the top because it comes with the territory. If you feel lonely in your position as a leader, then your leadership is all about your position and not about your people.

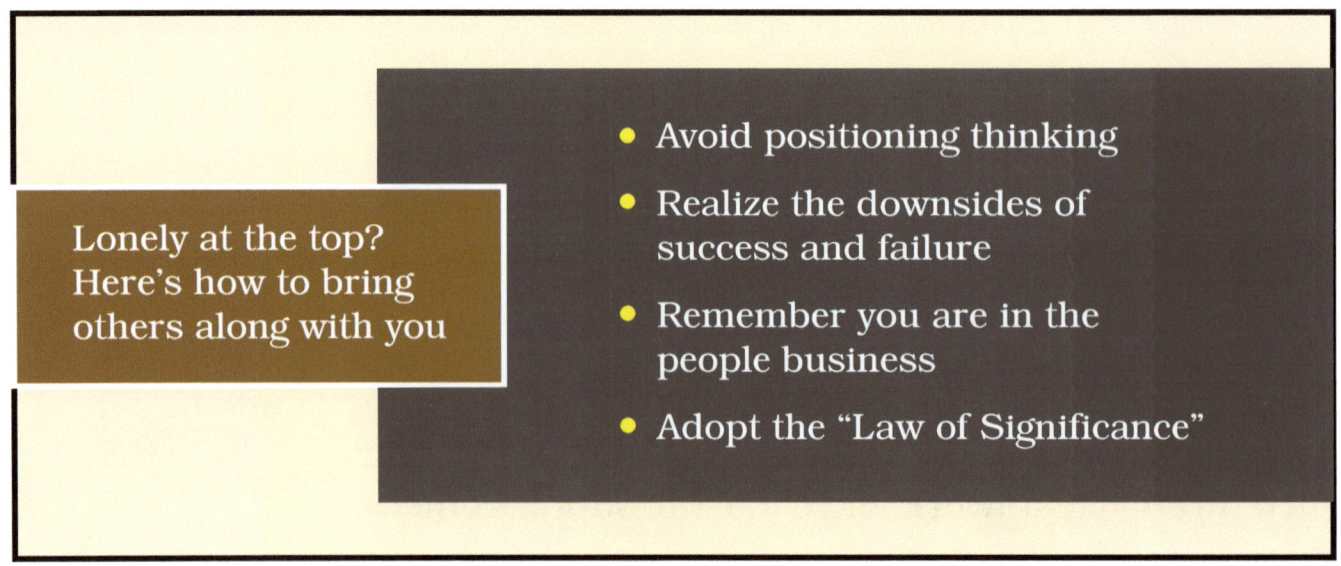

Lonely at the top? Here's how to bring others along with you

- Avoid positioning thinking
- Realize the downsides of success and failure
- Remember you are in the people business
- Adopt the "Law of Significance"

It is safe to conclude that if you are all alone then no one is following you. If no one is following you, you are just taking a walk. And if you are just taking a walk, then you're not really leading at all.

Question: How do I bring others along with me?

1. Avoid positional thinking.
   When you resort to using your status as a leader to intimidate your team members into producing results, you unwittingly create distance between you and them. Some call that maintaining a "power distance" and view it as a positive attribute. The truth is that a true leader does not belittle their people. On the contrary, they expand the horizon of their people. You must win your team members over by building relationships with them. Do that successfully and you will never be lonely.

2. Realize the downsides of success and failure.
   Success is just as dangerous to a leader as failure is. If you have started to record success, you may be tempted to believe you don't need your team. Ironically, they are the ones who helped you get there.

3. Always remember that you are in the people business. People are a resource and they have to be treated as such. They need attention, guidance and maintenance.

4. Adopt the Law of Significance which says: "One is too small of a number to achieve greatness." (John Maxwell's 17 Indispensable Laws of Teamwork)

You will be hard pressed to find anyone who made a significant impact as a leader all by themselves. Greatness is always bigger than what anyone can achieve all by themselves.

8.2 How to Lead Yourself

The narrative here is driven by a few questions.

Question: Do you have to interact with difficult people on your team?

Question: How do you lead such difficult team members?

Consider these important points:

1. The person you probably have the most difficult time leading is yourself
2. It is a full-time job to keep yourself motivated, maintain personal discipline and protect your integrity amongst other things.

The list is endless.

Question: Why do we find self-leadership so challenging?

There are two main reasons why self-leadership is challenging:

1. We seldom see ourselves as we see others. We therefore tend to demand higher standards from others than we do of ourselves. In other words, we are not evaluating our deliveries as leaders using the same standards applied to our team members.
2. Most people lack awareness that the human nature is equipped to assess everyone else except itself. This is why we are quick to judge and condemn other persons' deliveries.

In addition, we tend to judge others according to their actions. The process we adopt in our evaluations often leaves no room for flexibility. It's very cut and dried.

On the flip side, we judge ourselves by our intentions. The difference lies in the fact that even when we are in error, we excuse ourselves by saying we "had good intentions". It is to be noted the *"road to failure and ultimate disaster is paved with good intentions"*.

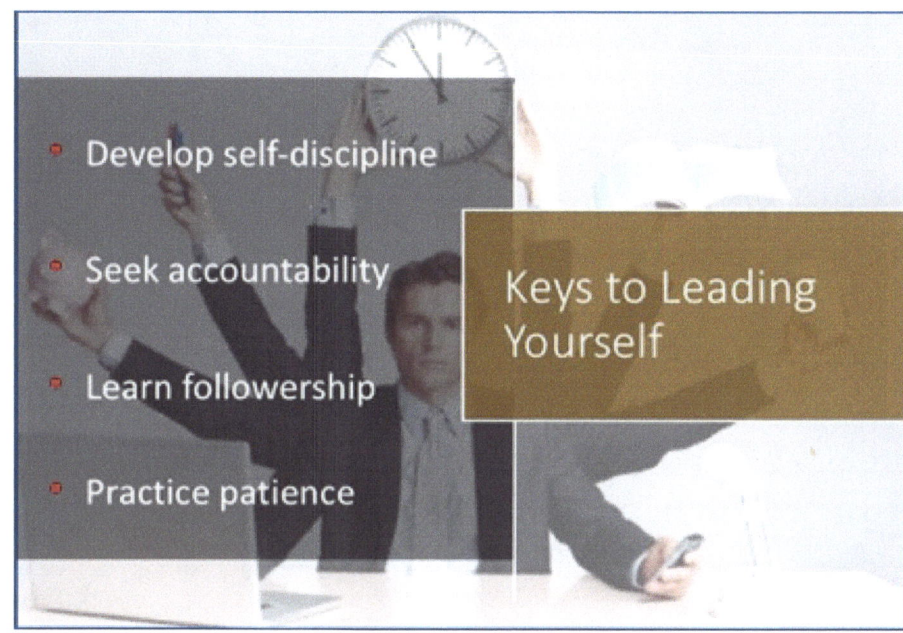

Question: How can I lead myself?

1. Develop self-discipline.

    There is a story about Frederick the Great of Prussia which helps to illustrate the art of self-discipline. One day, the King was taking a walk on the outskirts of Berlin when he encountered a very old man who was walking head and shoulders high in the opposite direction. "Who are you?" Frederick asked the old man who was actually his subject. "I am a king," replied the old man. "A king!" laughed Frederick. "Over what kingdom do you reign?" "Over myself," the proud old man replied.

    Discipline is simply giving yourself a command and following it through. It is the highest form of leadership. In this mode, you are the captain of your ship, the master of your own soul. Leading yourself is a challenge and one of the places where your true character shows up is in how you fare. There are days when you simply want to take a break from keeping yourself under control. Don't do it just because you feel like it.

2. Seek accountability.

   People who lead themselves well know a secret: they can't trust themselves. It is when you think you are untouchable that you learn how quickly you can be touched by poor choices.

   Question: Do you have an accountability partner or peer group?

   Personally, just being aware of an upcoming assignment such as putting finishing touches to a new book compels me to think and act straight.

   "Nothing so conclusively proves a man's ability to lead others, as what he does from day to day to lead himself." This statement is credited to Thomas Watson, a leading self-made industrialist and one of the richest men of his time. Probably most noted for his achievements as Chief Executive of International Business Machines (IBM), he was also referred to as the world's greatest salesman.

3. Learn followership. This is not quite as difficult as it seems. As a matter of fact, if you are effectively leading yourself, then you are already a good follower.

4. Learn patience. You will need a lot of it.

This section would be incomplete if we did not mention the power of the choices we make as leaders. Oftentimes, it is the choices we make in times of crisis that define us and shape our leadership style. If you desire to gain influence with people, then be a solution provider in all circumstances. This is where leadership becomes complicated. How you act or fail to act reveals to others just what your leadership competencies are.

Question: How do you react when facing a personal failure, when taking a stand on an issue, when experiencing suffering, or making an unpleasant choice?

All these and more, depending on how they are handled, can either move you forward or destroy your credibility, integrity and effectiveness.

8.3 How to Handle Criticism

It is safe to conclude that no one really loves being criticised. The paradox here is that this is one of the most certain experiences of a true leader. A true leader gets criticised all the time!

Every leader has a target on his or her back. The real question therefore is "how do you handle criticism?" Let us look a bit deeper into the subject and the relevance of criticism based on the moral of the following story.

A salesman mentioned to his barber that he was about to take a trip to Rome in Italy. "Rome is a terribly overrated city," commented his barber who was born in Northern Italy. "What airline are you taking?" The salesman told him the name of the airline and the barber responded, "What a terrible airline! Their seats are cramped, their food is bad, and their planes are always late. What hotel are you staying at?" The salesman named the hotel, and the barber explained, "Why would you stay there? That hotel is in the wrong part of town, and has horrible service. You're better off staying at home." "But I expect to close a big deal while I am there," the salesman replied. "And afterward I hope to see the

Pope." "You'll be disappointed trying to do business in Italy," said the barber. "Don't count on seeing the Pope too. He only grants audiences to very important people."

Three weeks later the salesman returned to the salon. "And how was your trip?" asked the barber. "Wonderful," replied the salesman. "The flight was perfect, the service at the hotel was excellent, and I made a big sale. "And" (the salesman paused for effect) "I got to meet the Pope." "You got to meet the Pope?" Finally, the barber was impressed. "Tell me what happened!" "Well, when I approached him, I bent down and kissed his ring." "No kidding! And what did he say?" "He looked down at my head and said, "My son, where did you get such a lousy haircut?"

People can change for the better only when they are open to improvement. How you handle criticism is vital to your growth as a leader. When you are criticised, try to maintain the right attitude by:

- Not being defensive
- Looking for the grain of truth
- Making the necessary changes
- Choosing to focus on the benefits

When you sit in the leader's seat, criticism finds your desk. Whether it is legitimate or not, maintain a positive attitude that there is gold in that pile of dirt. Below are some suggested questions to determine what kind of criticism you are getting.

Question: Who criticised you?

Adverse criticism from a wise person is more to be desired than the enthusiastic approval of a fool. The source often matters.

Question: How was the criticism given?

Try to discern whether the person was being judgmental or whether they gave you the benefit of the doubt and spoke with kindness.

Question: Why was the criticism given?

Was it given out of a personal grievance or for your benefit? Whether the criticism is legitimate or not, your attitude determines whether you derive any benefit from it.

8.4   The Leader's First Responsibility

Love what you do and you'll never work a single day in your life

WE SHALL HARNESS WHAT WE NEED TO SUSTAIN HUMAN EXISTENCE TODAY, BUT WE MUST PRESERVE SOMETHING FOR GENERATIONS TO COME.
OLUJIDE A. OJO (NIGERIA)

A leader's first responsibility is to have a passion for what they do. Following your passion is the key to finding your potential.

Question: How do you find your passion?

What you have a passion for can be identified by answering this simple question: "What do you love doing so much that you would do it for free?"

"A master in the art of living draws no sharp distinction between his work and his play; his labour and his leisure; his mind and his body; his education and his recreation. He hardly knows which is which. He simply pursues his vision of excellence through whatever he is doing, and leaves others to determine whether he is working or playing. To himself, he always appears to be doing both." - L.P. Jacks

Lawrence Pearsall Jacks (1860-1955) was an English educator, philosopher, and Unitarian minister who rose to prominence in the period from World War I to World War II.

If you feel Jacks' era and its philosophies are not so relevant in contemporary times, here's what Jack Welch has to say on the subject: "The world will belong to passionate, driven leaders ... people who not only have enormous amounts of energy, but who can energize those whom they lead."

Jack Welch is a retired business executive. He was Chairman and Chief Executive of General Electric (GE) from 1981 to 2001. During his tenure, the company's value rose 4,000%. In 2006, Welch's net worth was an estimated $720 million. When he retired from GE, he received a severance payment of $417 million, the largest such payment in history.

The core lesson learnt about passion from such great entrepreneurs is that people gravitate towards passion. It is a vibrant and constructive energy which attracts. Leadership is influence, nothing more, nothing less.

Question: Are you passionate about the work you do?

Perhaps you need a reality check in order to find what is real. This may not necessarily be within your immediate sphere of influence. For example, I once held a position as Chief Operating Officer for one of the leading Nigerian independents. Being in that position provided me access to the Chief Executive, close enough to feel his passion and to perceive his vision for the company. Though he was focussed on the vision, he exhibited one major flaw: he never wanted to hear bad news about what was happening.

If you are not able to hear both the good and the bad, then you are not carrying out one of the major responsibilities of a leader. It is a leader's job to define reality. One of the pitfalls that can stop you as a potential leader is the desire to focus on the vision and fail to face reality.

Question: How do I find what is real?

The simple answer is to do a reality check. This can be achieved in four (4) simple steps:

1. Be aware of your weaknesses. No one is perfect. Your team probably already knows your weaknesses. Admitting that you are NOT a superhero merely confirms to your team that you are aware of that fact.

2. Embrace realistic people. Birds of a feather do flock together. As much as is within your purview to determine your team's composition, always have members whose strengths complement the apparent weaknesses.

3. Encourage honest and open feedback from others to you. That will keep you grounded. As the boss, it becomes more difficult to have people around tell you what you need to hear rather than what you want to hear.

4. Invite fresh eyes to check you out. Jim Collins in Good to Great says: "You absolutely cannot make a series of good decisions without first confronting the brutal facts."

Good leaders who lead great companies face reality and make changes accordingly.

8.5 Leaders Never Stop Learning

Leaders learn continually.

Question: Do you have a personal growth plan?

You have taken a good first step by getting this book. However, true leadership development happens over a period of time. It is a process and the question really is "What are you doing every day to develop as a leader?" A book like this can make you aware of what you need to do to develop as a leader but, at best, it can only be the start of the learning process.

Question: How much have you invested in your personal growth in the past six (6) to 12 months?

Experts tell us we should be spending 10% of our income investing in personal development. To sustain the effort to keep learning and growing, the idea of having a personal theme for the year works for most. One-word themes such as PERSISTENCE and INTENTIONAL keep the leader focused on what direction they want their personal and business life to go. "To grow, you have to be intentional." – John Maxwell

Question: How do I keep learning and growing?

1. Invest in yourself first. There is a direct link between how your company grows and how you grow.
2. If you want to lead, you must learn. If you want to continue to lead, you must continue to learn.
3. Create a growth environment for the people you lead.

In closing this section, let us consider what a growth environment (item 3 above) looks like. Consider the following 10 characteristics.

A growth environment is a place where:

1.   Others are ahead of you
2.   You are continually challenged
3.   Your focus is forward
4.   The atmosphere is affirming
5.   You are often out of your comfort zone
6.   You wake up excited
7.   Failure is not your enemy
8.   Others are growing
9.   People desire change
10. Growth is modelled and expected

If you can create a growth environment, people in your organisation will grow and improve. High potential individuals will desire to be part of your team and your organisation will be transformed.

8.6 How to be a Leader Worth Following

The first thing a leader must be aware of regarding the dynamics of human capital turnover is that people quit people, not companies.

"Some cause happiness wherever they go. Some cause happiness whenever they go." - Oscar Wilde (Irish poet and playwright)

Some sources estimate that as many as 65% of people leaving companies do so because of their managers. We may say that people quit their job or their company, but the reality is that they usually no longer want to be in the same space as their leaders.

The 'company' does not do anything negative to them but people do. Sometimes co-workers cause the problems that prompt people to leave. But the people who often alienate employees are their direct supervisors.

Question: What type of people do employees avoid?

1. People avoid leaders who devalue them. Such bosses manipulate and start treating them like objects. That is never appropriate for any leader. A leader should rather appreciate their team, find out where they add value and place them there to maximize their efforts.

2. People quit people who are untrustworthy. "Effective leaders ensure that people feel strong and capable" - Michael Winston (erstwhile Chief Executive for Countrywide Financial Corporation). Trust in the leader is essential if other people are going to follow that person over time.

   People must see that the leader is believable, credible, and trustworthy. Trust in the leader or any other person is developed through consistency in behaviour, when words and deeds are congruent.

   Some of the quickest ways leaders lose the trust of their people are:

   - Acting inconsistently in what they say and do
   - Seeking personal gain above shared gain
   - Withholding information
   - Lying or telling half-truths
   - Being close-minded

3. People avoid leaders who are incompetent

4. People avoid leaders who are insecure

8.7 Leadership Legacy

There are four (4) ways to become a leader worth following rather than one who keeps losing key people.

1. Take responsibility for relationships. As a leader, you must take the lead in making sure relationships are positively oriented. Value those who work for you. It is wonderful when the people believe in their leader. It is even more wonderful when the leader believes in the people.

2. Prioritise credibility. As a leader, there will be times when you are overwhelmed. During these times, maintain credibility.

3. Maintain positive emotional health. Follow the golden rule and have a positive attitude with your team. It will be contagious. That is the bug you want your people to catch.

4. Lastly, maintain a teachable spirit. Understand that everyone and every situation can teach you something. Having this posture with your team will encourage them to desire same. Remember, people do what people see.

If people still insist on leaving having done all you can to stop them, always conduct exit interviews. Find out if you are the reason they are leaving and if you are, take the high road and own it.

People will summarise your life in one sentence. Pick that statement yourself now. What would you like to be remembered for?

American author and politician, and first woman to hold a major U.S. ambassadorial post, Clare Boothe Luce called this your "life sentence." If you are intentional about creating a legacy, people won't have to wonder what your life sentence is.

Eleanor Roosevelt had this to say; "Life is like a parachute jump. You've got to get it right the first time." She was a renowned American political figure, diplomat and activist, First Lady of the United States of America for three (3) consecutive terms (1933-1945).

Author and leadership expert, John Kotte, said "Most people don't lead their lives; they just accept them." Don't allow that statement to apply to you. Begin choosing the legacy you want to leave now. It may be just the beginning of the process, but that's okay. You must start in order to finish.

In closing the final section of this book, here is some advice from the author, Jide Akindele-Ojo: "Watch life unfold as you embrace change. Make the right choices."

Thank you for letting us be a part of your professional growth and development. We trust it has been as exciting for you as it has been rewarding for us in delivering this.